WOMEN NOT WANTED

WOMEN NOT WANTED

ONE FEMALE OFFICER AND HER JOURNEY FOR JUSTICE

BY

SHERRY LEE BENSON-PODOLCHUK

Copyright 2007 by Sherry Lee Benson-Podolchuk

First Edition 2007
Second Printing 2010

Printed on Recycled Paper
Book Cover by Tetro Design Incorporated
Cover Photo by Ian McCausland
Printed by Hignell Book Printing, Winnipeg, Canada
Library and Archives Canada Cataloguing in Publication
Benson-Podolchuk, Sherry Lee, 1962-
Women not wanted: one RCMP officer and her journey for justice /
Sherry Lee Benson-Podolchuk.

ISBN 978-0-9784211-3-7

1. Benson-Podolchuk, Sherry Lee, 1962-
2. Sexual harassment in law enforcement--Canada.
3. Discrimination in law enforcement--Canada.
4. Royal Canadian Mounted Police--Biography.
5. Policewomen-- Canada--Biography.
I. Title.

HV7911.B45A3 2007

363.2082'092   C2007-906661-5

Note to Readers

This is an account of my twenty years as a female officer with the Royal Canadian Mounted Police. I wrote this book in order to deal with the traumatic events of my tenure with the RCMP and to heal my own wounds from the years of workplace conflict.

Women were first allowed to join the RCMP as regular officers in 1974 and have played an increasing role within the Force since then. The first all-female troop graduated March 3, 1975. However, at that time, while elsewhere in society there were policies against sexual harassment, in the RCMP there were none. Despite recent changes within the Force, there continues even today to be a struggle with harassment and discrimination. Historically, it has taken many years for women to reach the higher ranks within the RCMP. To date women make up 17% of RCMP police officers. To those officers who have had successful, fulfilling and harassment-free careers, congratulations.

In writing this account, it was imperative that I release the pain from my soul and onto paper. Through therapy, I learned to take responsibility for my choices and not for the actions of others. My experiences as a victim in a male-dominated bureaucracy are not unique. As a single mother on welfare, I struggled to find a better life for my child and myself, and this is evidence that people can change the direction of their lives by finding the courage and strength within themselves. If the pain and suffering I have endured can bring comfort and hope to others for a better life, then with this book I have achieved a worthwhile goal. When I first joined the RCMP in 1989 with the hopes of a long and successful career, I had no idea at the time that my career would be marred with sexual harassment and discrimination. Simply put, it has been an enlightening experience.

"My power is my voice - actively challenging the harassment and abuse of power in the workplace through encouragement, education and accountability."

This story is based on my experiences and perspective of events; names and places have been changed to protect the legal rights of those involved as well as to maintain confidentiality for the innocent.

TO

Nadine

MY INSPIRATION TO BUILD
A BETTER LIFE

Acknowledgements

I would like to acknowledge the following people: my therapist and anchor; the Benson family: Harvey, Sylvia, Brad, Bennetta, Tanis, Bruce, Kim and Eric, their spouses and children; Isabella Ayers who gave me the gift of baking; the Podolchuk family: Elaine, Irene, Ivan, Alan, their spouses and children for welcoming me into the family; Dr. Wray and Allie Pascoe for the weekly coffee chats and continued support. I would also like to acknowledge the Good-Bye Girls (you know who you are). I love you all. The staff at the Kaffe Haus which provided the much needed cups of coffee tover the many years. Superintendent A --- who gave me encouraging words when I applied to the RCMP. Brian and Milena, your friendship is a blessing. Our B.C. buddies, Phil, Usta, Mark and Brenda: thanks for the best view of Vancouver. Thank you Holly B. and Holly C. Neighbours and friends too numerous to mention. The men and women of Troop 6, I hope you had great careers. To all the people I have had the privilege to meet in the line of duty, thank you, you have enriched my life. I hope the feeling is mutual. To all the frontline police officers I have known, keep up the good work. To Lois Spellman who was kind, gracious and patient to edit my many drafts. To Kate B. for editing the second print. The wonderful work done by Tétro Design for their creative ideas.

A special thanks to John for his support over the years. Thanks to Darryl Buxton and Garth Smorang, my legal team. Respectful thanks to the late Honorable Ron Duhamel who was willing to bring my fight to Parliament. To my darling daughter Nadine, who has been, and continues to be, an inspiration to me. For you, my Tweety, I never gave up the fight for justice. Finally, beloved David, husband, lover and best friend. Thank you for keeping me grounded and for giving me the stars. I love you.

Five years old and ready to take on the world.

LEFT: April 24, 1989. 06:00 at my apartment in Gimli and getting ready to leave for D Division to be sworn in as an officer of the RCMP. It was the hardest day of my life, leaving Nadine for six months, the agony of not knowing when I would be back and if she would forget me. I kept thinking the six months out of a lifetime is only a blink

BOTTOM LEFT: In the RCMP women's barracks at Regina Saskatchewan. Straight sheets and blankets, polished floor, holster, gun belt, and clean hat. Perfectly ironed shirt and skirt and look at those shoes.

RIGHT: 1989 Looking forward to a new career with the RCMP.

BOTTOM RIGHT: Leaving for a night shift during the summer months at Tisdale Detachment but not before getting a good night kiss from Nadine.

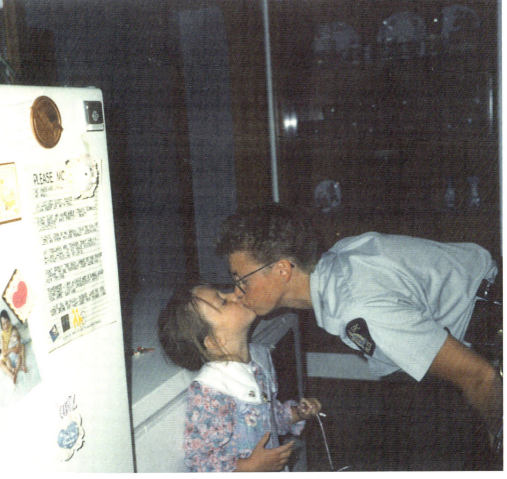

TOP: June 24, 2009. This photo represents all my years of struggle. Twenty years and beyond. I made it to this pinnacle point of my RCMP career. Twenty years of blood, sweat and many tears. I earned my place among the other dedicated officers. (PHOTO TAKEN BY HOLLY PENNER)

RIGHT: 2009 Survived the twenty years. Thankful and moving forward with the lessons learned

BOTTOM: I enjoyed celebrating my 'moon landing experience' with family and friends. Sharing this moment with Nadine and Auntie Allie who lovingly christened me 'The Queen of Light'. Removing the memory of the RCMP's name Princess of Darkness. One journey over and more wonderful adventures just ahead. My future is dedicated to help empower women to find their voice. (PHOTO TAKEN HOLLY PENNER.)

Foward
"Women NOT WANTED"
ABOUT THE WRITER

Marilyn J. MacKenzie was appointed in 1985 by the University of Manitoba as the first university Sexual Harassment Investigation Officer in Canada.

Ms MacKenzie is an influential and recognized authority on the implementation of morally and ethically correct policy for major businesses, governments, and higher learning institutions, and is a pioneer in the field of discrimination and harassment, prevention and elimination. Her other credits include:

Twice President and Past President of the *Canadian Association Against Sexual Harassment in Higher Education*

Founding member of *Manitoba Professionals Against Discrimination and Harassment in the Workplace*

First Canadian recipient of *"In the Trenches" award* presented by the *Safe Schools of America Coalition Against Sexual Assault and Harassment*

Woman of the Year, and of Distinction, Nominee 1984 and 1987

Investigated and mediated over 600 cases of discrimination and harassment throughout Canada and the United States

Delivered hundreds of Educational Sessions on the prevention and elimination of discrimination and harassment

Expert witness status

The Golden Rule
DO UNTO OTHERS AS YOU WOULD HAVE THEM DO UNTO YOU

Until we live in a perfect world where people conduct themselves in a manner respectful of others, and value differences and individuality - regardless of sex, race, sexual orientation, creed, religion, colour, disability, age, size, family or marital status, nationality, ancestry, or place of origin - until that time, there will always be a need for those who can point us in the right direction.

Discrimination, harassment, abuse of power, or bullying are often serious, hurtful and damaging. These prevalent behaviours affect the targets or victims psychologically, emotionally, and physically. Yet, despite the painful and humiliating experiences Sherry Lee suffered, she succeeds in presenting her materials in an entertaining manner. She often makes us laugh and feel her warmth and understanding of the vulnerability of those clients she served, as well as her own.

Harassers are classified as "benign", "anger based", or "hard core". It doesn't matter in which type of disrespectful, degrading or demeaning behaviour a harasser engages, their common characteristic is abusing power. Whether their behaviour comprises acts of racism, sexism, sexual harassment, homophobia or any other forms of discrimination, they will often seek out the vulnerable, people like Sherry who initially described herself as " a quiet person not able to stand up to someone who was domineering," and then they attack. Once the harasser locates his or her victim, the predator sets to work.

Fortunately, for Sherry, once she became aware of the assaults, she began the long and painful healing process, and with help and determination, she evolved from a victim to a survivor and, ultimately with the publishing of this book, she became a warrior.

Her recovery was indeed long and painful and not without set backs. She initially slips into a common trap of trying to "fit in," to be one of the "boys," condone certain behaviours, some which may initially feel like "good natured fun." Examples sited relate to her white teeth, earning her the nickname of "Constable Colgate," or "Chiclets". She also goes out for a few drinks and tries to fit in.

Sexual harassment is a "Catch 22". If one complains about a hand on the shoulder, the complainant is often labeled over reactive, super sensitive or perhaps emotionally unbalanced. However, if one remains silent and the behaviour expands to groping, fondling or sexual assault which eventually draws a complaint, the target may be accused of enticing the harasser or being a tease.

A female working in a male dominated environment is often subjected to continuous testing. Danger flags tend to spring up if a female demonstrates superior competence and intelligence. If these qualities are combined with integrity and the refusal to distort facts, or deceive, or participate in sexual banter, or accept sexual comments, or comply with sexual requests, it is likely such a person will not be considered a "team player."

For Sherry all the flags went up and were waved in her face. As a result of her refusal to comply, she suffered acts of reprisal ranging from the subtle to the severe. Old standing practices such as mileage records were scrutinized and she was an endangered species on several occasions.

No one should be exposed to the type of abuse which Sherry endured. However, discrimination in all its variations persists in many workplaces. Although policies and procedures are being formulated, and educational programs developed, the bullies continue to thrive.

It is Sherry's belief that her book will encourage others to come forward, identify and resist discrimination, harassment and abuse of power whenever and wherever they appear.

The financial costs to complacent institutions can often prompt them to become proactive in deterring these destructive behaviours. The human cost, however, is much greater. In my experience the effects are often devastating and in some cases are manifested in anxiety attacks, eating disorders, depression and loss of mental well being. Sherry is commended for her strength and commitment in her battle against this form of injustice. She has emerged as a survivor and will advance as an advocate and leader in her mission to ensure all individuals are treated with respect, dignity and equality. Her willingness to share her story will no doubt give strength and courage to others.

Marilyn MacKenzie, B.A., M.S.W

Preface
GETTING TO KNOW ME

In 2007 as I watched the television one evening, I felt pity for the Commissioner of the RCMP as he had to admit to the Justice Inquiry in Ottawa, that he had made a mistake in his previous testimony on the RCMP Pension issue. Within a few days he had resigned. In my mind, however, it was his manner of management that had allowed the corruption of senior officers to exist and persist, and as a result of this failure in management, harassment discrimination and abuse of power continued. I believe the many years of my enduring such torment is not an isolated incident.

My career began in 1989, when I joined the RCMP in Winnipeg, Manitoba and headed for Regina for six months of training. As a young child, I had always admired and respected the RCMP. Their job looked like fun. At that time, when I joined the RCMP, I was a single mother with an 18-month-old daughter, and becoming a police officer was not a romantic fantasy but simply the result of listening to advice of my older sister, Bennetta. When she was attending university in the early 1980's, she suggested that if I wanted good money, I should acquire a job that was in a male dominated field and I listened to her.

I am the fifth child of a large family of seven children. I was a tiger as a small child, teasing my siblings to the point of madness. I would lie on the couch kicking my legs so fast that it was impossible for anyone to get a hit. My father was the principal of my high school. His greatest gift to me was a love of exercise and that this should be a lifestyle. I can recall when I was twelve and chubby, being chased around the track with my dad behind me, every once in a while giving me a gentle tap to keep going. Exercise continues to be a part of my life. My mother was a qualified teacher but most of my life, a stay-at-home mom. She showed me how make birthdays, Christmas and other celebrations and holidays special. Although she was busy and tired raising the seven children, I admired her spirit and ability to get a job done. She made an effort to make daily life fun by having homegrown (from our garden) tomato sandwiches for lunches in the fall, pancake Fridays and hamburger nights. In our family there was encouragement as to the importance of education and self-determination, and this was important to all the kids. Our home was filled with the smells of home baked goods. Mom wanted me to be a Home Economics teacher and Dad wanted me to be a nurse. I surprised them both.

My first contact with the RCMP was in my early teens while playing knock-knock ginger. A game where you ring doorbells in the middle of the night, hide in the shadows and wait to see the people come to answer the door, then giggle and do it again. It was quite fun until the police pulled up into the driveway and used the police car spot light making us flee into the darkness. Unfortunately not being the athlete of today I could not keep up with the others. I watched them race across the snow covered empty lot unable to follow them to safety. I could hear the sound of a car door slam knowing one of the officers was out looking for us. The sound of footsteps behind gave me such terror knowing it was the RCMP on hot pursuit. I ran to the nearest yard not knowing if there was any place to find safety. Looking around saw a trailer silently parked in the back of the yard. Racing like a scared rabbit threw myself under the parked trailer and lay on my stomach hoping not to be discovered. Only the sound of my beating heart and pounding chest seemed to echo into the night. The crunching sound of snow broke the rhythm of my breathing and suddenly, I saw the black boots, yellow stripped pants standing directly in front of the trailer, only inches from my face. I am sure he can hear my breathing. Fear is powerful thing and I was frozen with fear. I seemed to die a thousand deaths in that instant regretting every doorbell I ever rang, praying to be spared, and promising to be good. I wondered if he could see any part of me sticking out from under the trailer and when he did not walk all the way around realized I was temporarily safe. As I watched, the boots disappear into the night waited until I was nearly frozen and then quietly rolled out from under the trailer. I listened carefully to any sound which would indicate the cops were on the move. Using the shadows of houses and trees slowly made my way home, and made sure not to cross near any streetlights. Several times the police car drove by and I again hid behind trees, cars, and in the ditches. Once home I crawled through an open window in the basement. My body was aching from the cold but mostly from the adrenaline. You would think that after this experience I would want nothing to do with the game of knock-knock ginger. Well, I became a better runner.

I graduated from the Gimli High School in 1981, and spent 13 months in Australia as a Rotary exchange student. I ate, drank and was very merry, returning to Canada 50 pounds heavier. I actually weighed one pound more than my Dad and once I got stuck in the tub. The first time I went jogging after Australia, I managed to run one block and thought I was having a heart attack. I was so upset, I walked back to the house and ate a bag of Oreo cookies. That is 40 cookies. I did not give up on running and it took years of determination to get my body back to the pre-exchange student weight.

In the fall of 1982, I was employed at the Elementary School as a Librarian Assistant, and there I met a young RCMP officer from Quebec, his name was John, who was just out of the Training Academy. As English was his second language, communication could have been difficult, but we managed to understand each other. He was funny, and being young, we fell in love. During the 5 years we were together we moved to The Pas, Manitoba, in 1985, which is located some 400 kilometers north of Winnipeg.

I landed a job as a bank teller and enjoyed working with the public. In November of 1986 I noticed that I was feeling nauseated and went to a Physician. I was pregnant. The next three months I struggled with morning sickness twenty-four hours a day but continued to work at the bank. It was difficult not to get sick from various smells, especially smoke. For example, at that time people could smoke in public places and while standing in line. The smoke bothered me more after becoming pregnant. I would start to gag at the smell of cigars. As the bank was close to my home, I would go home for lunch. If John had a day off or was working nights, he would sometimes make lunch for us. One day John made a surprise lunch. I opened the front door, smelled the pepperoni, cheese and mushroom omelet, turned around and promptly threw up on the porch. I did not have the stomach to enter the house until all the windows were open to get rid of the smell. He was angry that I didn't try to eat it. Another day he made rabbit stew the smell was horrible, similar to wet sport socks. Eventually, after a few months the morning sickness lessened. The first time I felt my precious baby was March 5, 1987. I was at a friend's place and felt this flutter in my stomach, like I had swallowed a butterfly. This was so exciting! As the months wore on and my belly got bigger, I fell in love with the tiny presence moving around inside me. Despite the joy of having a baby, I also noticed that my relationship with John was not going the way I wanted.

On August 2 1987 I had a baby girl. The first thing I noticed about her was her blue eyes and long fingers. Together John and I enjoyed our new addition but the connection between us was different. After a few months we decided to part. I needed to grow on my own, as I had found the relationship oppressive. I was a quiet person and not able to stand up to someone who was domineering. We both had to grow, and being apart seemed the best solution. Sometimes people mature after a relationship ends. I hoped this would be the case for me.

In the winter of 1988 baby Nadine and I moved to Gimli. As I had no formal education and limited job skills, I applied for Provincial Welfare to support my child while I applied for positions in the local banks, and eventually, I was hired at the Gimli Credit Union. However, after working two weeks and collecting my pay cheque I was disappointed to learn that whatever money I earned would be deducted from the welfare amount, so once the babysitter was paid, I was making less than if I had not worked.

I was thankful my grandmother and I would shop together. She spent $40 a week on groceries for Nadine and I, plus buy my lunch. Although I struggled financially, John did pay for various things that were needed, and he remains in our lives as my best supporter. He sent monthly cheques to help with the cost of raising a child.

During our five-year relationship, I met many RCMP officers, and realized what type of qualities and intelligence are required to join the RCMP. I compared my unique abilities to some of the officers and I knew if these men could be police officers, then with the proper training, I could be a great asset to the RCMP family.

At "D" Division in Winnipeg I completed an application. It took several months of waiting and I was eventually accepted. The physical test was easy, a few pushups, sit-ups and a step test and since I was in good physical condition, had little difficulty. I was notified I would be officially sworn in the RCMP on April 24, 1989 at "D" Division, and from there off to Montreal for six weeks of language training, then to Regina for six months. Perhaps my childhood memories of an interesting career could come true. I could hardly wait for the adventure to start.

Training Was Fun
But Not The Real World

FROM JUNE TO DECEMBER 1989 I ATTENDED THE RCMP'S Regina Training Academy, and discovered I really enjoyed the physical and mental challenges. My troop consisted of 22 women and 10 men. I knew it was going to be a mental game between the recruits and the Corporals who trained us in swimming, self defense, law, hazard pursuit driving and other related courses. The Corporals were always trying to get us to crack under pressure. One such instructor stands out, our Drill Instructor, Cpl. Bob Wooden. We would line up in perfect order and stand rigidly to attention, ready for his inspection. Cpl. Wooden would slowly walk up each row and inspect our uniform, looking for 'invisible dust' so he had a reason to yell and scream or make us do 'ten-to-ones'. 'Ten-to-ones' is a torture which has you run back and forth to each end of the large parade square, do ten pushups, then nine and so on down to one. The secret was not to draw attention to yourself, at all, during the six months in Depot.

I pretty much blew the first day of drill practice. Cpl. Wooden was slowly moving along the line toward me and suddenly I felt like giggling. Sometimes when nervous, I laugh. I knew if I laughed, that was it, I was doomed to torture for the six months. Sure enough, as Cpl. Wooden came into my view, I crossed my eyes so as not to laugh, stood rigid and stared straight ahead. He stopped and gazed into my face, waiting, as my eyes slowly focused on him. I could not help my-self. I smiled, one of my biggest smiles. His response surprised me: "Constable Benson, don't smile like that, you are blinding me." He spoke in a loud long drawn out voice, but there was a hint of humour in his eyes. I started to laugh. "Give me 'ten-to-ones', and don't get back in line until you can stop laughing. Now break ranks." I left my line, laughing and began to run back and forth in the drill hall. There were some other quiet giggles among the troop but when Cpl. Wooden walked up and down the line, all went quiet, except for me. I kept laughing the entire time, out of fear. I had the giggles. Once finished laughing and the ten-to-ones, I approached the line to resume my position in the inspection. Cpl. Wooden turned and walked toward me. He looked so serious that even though I was exhausted, I smiled again, and giggled.

"Constable Benson, I don't think you understood my last request. Give me 'ten-to-ones' and don't come back into line until you have stopped laughing."

I began another set of ten to ones. Finally, after over 120 push-ups and miles of running, I staggered back to the inspection line, not laughing. Everyone was standing at attention and waiting for me. Cpl. Wooden approached me as I stood in line, looked at my red face, my chest heaving with fatigue and my uniform all out of place, then he rolled his eyes and moved so close to my face our noses were almost touching. So far I had managed to keep a straight face but he held my gaze, then I started to laugh. He took his drill stick, banged it on the floor and addressed the rest of the troop. Everyone was terrified, especially me.

His voice boomed and echoed throughout the drill hall, "We have a problem here, Constable Benson wants to do 'ten-to-ones' again but

I am not going make you all stand and wait, so class dismissed except for Benson." There were practically skid marks on the floor as the rest of the troop raced for the exit. I stood there, alone, with my big smile just looking at the man who was going to make me do pushups until I puked. I was angry because I could not stop smiling even when I was terrified. Cpl. Wooden waited for the class to leave the building, turned and walked in front of me with a very serious face. I got scared, thinking 'Oh God, another set. I am in trouble; he is going to make my life a living hell for six months. I need to quit giggling.'

I stood alone, facing Cpl. Wooden, trying to not breathe loudly, my nostrils flaring like an angry bull. He simply smiled as I stood stiff, erect, and while he paced slowly around me he began abruptly asking questions. "Constable Benson, why are you here?"

"I am here to get a rewarding career and support my baby daughter, Corporal." I stood at attention while addressing my superior.

Gasping for breath, I had answered quickly as he did not give me time to think about what I thought he wanted to hear. I couldn't seem to catch my breath and made some choking sounds.

I was pleasantly surprised when he stopped in front of me and said with a smile, "Well, Benson, let's just say you owe me a set of ten-to-ones. Dismissed." For a split second I thought he was joking. I had escaped my third set of torture for today. I knew the 'No smiling' part in drill was going to be difficult for me as I had practiced not smiling prior to coming to Regina but had failed miserably.

Needless to say, every drill class, I smiled during troop inspection and had to do 'ten-to-ones' for the entire six months. By the end of training I could stand, drop to my hands, do the pushups and not scratch my drill boots. I was extremely fit, my arms and legs firm and muscular.

During the six months of training, I became known as 'Constable Colgate' or 'Chiclets' because of my big smile. I have large front teeth and the other instructors would tease me as I walked from class to class. Some of the Corporals would yell, "Constable Benson, stop smiling, the sun is shining off your teeth and blinding me." So much for remaining anonymous.

During training, I gained friendships from within our troop and from among the staff and some of the friendly Corporals. Training was hard because of the early hours and the intensive physical training and drill sessions. In self defense class, one of the Corporals looked at my arms, which were long, and said that I needed, "to eat two desserts today to get some meat on my arms," and I was a 'train killer.' The statement was dripping with sarcasm. I thought, 'Is he saying I am skinny, or that I have muscles?' I did not know if this was a compliment or an insult, but either way, I worked hard at learning the different self defense techniques. Despite all the pushups I was never able to look hulking with my five foot six inch, one hundred thirty five pound frame.

On graduation day in December 1989 I was acknowledged, by the troops and staff, as the friendliest person in the depot, which was an honour. I hoped the rest of my service in the RCMP would be filled with such kindness and friendship. My parents, grandmother, sister Kim, her boyfriend and Nadine attended the graduation. I was still in fantasy land.

My First Detachment, My First Day, My First Accident

MY FIRST ASSIGNMENT WAS IN TISDALE, A SMALL TOWN in Saskatchewan. As I drove into the town late in the evening of my arrival with my little girl, my sister and my mom, I can still remember my reaction: 'My my what a small town, what kind of town have I brought my daughter to?' I had a feeling that finding childcare would be complicated for the two years I was to be at this detachment. Joining the RCMP and taking Nadine to Tisdale as a single mom was a huge step. I knew raising her would be difficult, with shift work and my being called out at all hours, but I had decided to raise Nadine myself, and her dad agreed. I also knew I had to give it a chance, and hindsight has shown my first reaction was accurate. It was a small detachment consisting of a Sergeant, two Corporals and six Constables.

The first year was uneventful in terms of major crimes, nevertheless it was filled with a many 'firsts'. My first official day wearing the RCMP uniform was February 14, 1990. I have a photo of how happy I was at the beginning of my service, with high hopes for a great career. My supervisor Sergeant Chilton met me at the front door when I arrived at the detachment, a red brick building with limited windows. After giving me a brief tour of the detachment and introductions to the staff, he asked me to drive him to Melfort to pick up office supplies. The town was about 30 kilometers from Tisdale, and I was nervous driving this tall, burly, deep-voiced man who was also three ranks above me. This fear came from brainwashing in training: 'all ranks above low-life constables are to be revered'. In training any person who dared question the order of a Corporal was punished with extra duties, confined to base for the weekend or humiliated in front of the troop. We chatted about the policing in a small town, the various types of crimes and the shifts involved. After our return from Melfort, I left Sergeant Chilton at the office and went home for lunch.

It was great to see Nadine and how happy she seemed to be in our new home. My sister and my mom had agreed to stay with me in Tisdale a little longer while I made arrangements for childcare.

When I was heading back to the detachment that afternoon, a car backed out of a driveway directly in my path. I slammed on the brakes but hit dead center, smashing both the passenger side doors. As you can imagine, there was a sinking sensation in my stomach. This was my first day. Fortunately, there was only a tiny scratch to the chrome front bumper of the police car. The driver of the other car was not hurt and took complete responsibility for not looking. I could see the front door of the detachment and to add insult to injury, I had to radio Sergeant Chilton. "Sergeant Chilton Alpha 5." That is the code for the detachment car number.

"Go ahead Alpha 5," responded the deep voice.

"I don't know how to say this, but I just got in an accident. The other driver is walking to the detachment to complete the accident forms."

There was a long pause, and a sense of impending doom overcame my happy feeling.

"Where did the accident happen?"

"Look outside the front window, and you can see me waving."

I sheepishly waved as three people came into view; one of them was Sergeant Chilton, holding the police radio.

"Come back to the office, Alpha 5"

I could scarcely believe this was happening, and I so wanted to make a good impression, not to screw up in the first four hours of my first shift! I entered with a heavy heart, yet determined to take whatever discipline might be coming in order to move on from this disastrous first day. To my surprise, I was met with laughter - the secretaries and all the officers were laughing. The other driver had just left after completing the necessary accident forms.

Sergeant Chilton looked at me with a big grin, "Any damage to the police car?'

From my lips came a tiny sound. "No."

"You still have to complete the internal RCMP forms because of the amount of damage to the other car, however, it was clearly the other driver's fault. This is your first day, what are your plans for tomorrow?" Everyone laughed except me. My face flushed from embarrassment and fear. I could only manage a smile.

My field-training officer in Tisdale was Corporal Mat, who was just about to retire with over 30 years in the RCMP. He left me alone for most of the time while we were working together I don't know if that was intentional or just absentmindedness.

I fumbled along as best I could for my first few months, making many mistakes in completing the various forms and other paperwork in required in police work. For example, my first traffic stop was for a driver not wearing his seatbelt. While writing out the ticket, I was so nervous I had to write it out three times just to ensure there were no errors. By the time the ticket was completed and I had walked up to the driver's side, I noticed he had been reading a book during the whole time. He simply smiled at my embarrassment on issuing him the summons and explaining the process of payment. We both had a good laugh. Eventually, with practice, the nervousness was replaced with confidence in my ability. By the next year, this same driver and I had become friends and laughed over this incident.

One dayshift Corporal Mat and I were to arrest a person, Luke Bernard, under the Mental Health Act. Luke's family had made application for his arrest as he was not taking his medication, not eating, and they feared for his own safety. This was my first opportunity to use the training I had learned regarding entering a home where there is a possibility of violence. I asked my superiors questions, "What do I say to the suspect upon entering the house?" "Do we say we want to talk to him to gain his trust then once in the house make the arrest?" "What happens if he goes into another room should I follow?" Corporal Mat indicated this would be quick and easy as he and Luke knew each other from previous police altercations. During the drive my heart was pumping frantically, my brain wondering which self-defense control techniques to use. Although Corporal Mat had years of experience and he knew the suspect, he decided to stand directly in front of the doorway. This is unsafe as a suspect could fire through the door killing the police officer on the other side. I was confused.

"Corporal do you think we should stand on the sides of the entrance? What if he shoots through the door?" I asked, aware of his rank and my own fear of offending him.

"No, not to worry, I know this guy, he is harmless," replied Corporal Mat.

I decided to follow my training and slowly moved to the side of the door. I did not want to be a statistic among officers who did not follow procedure and were shot. Corporal Mat knocked on the door while my mind was racing. What would happen if this guy has a gun? I did not want to die and leave Nadine alone.'

We heard some commotion at the door and a middle-aged man, short in stature, slowly opened the door a crack. He peered out and gave each of us glaring looks. I thought, 'He looks deranged and angry.' The man's head twitching, and wide eyes shifting back and forth.

Corporal Mat pushed at the door and instructed the suspect: "Open the door, Luke, we need to talk to you, Luke, I am here to arrest you."

At that point the fight was on. The door was slammed in Corporal Mat's face. He pushed into the house and Luke ran into the living room. All I could think was 'This guy is going to get a gun and kill us!' I followed closely as Corporal Mat chased Luke to the living room. Luke turned and grabbed at Corporal Mat. The two of them wrestled on the floor, stood up and fell onto the couch which tipped under their weight. I could see their feet up in the air as the couch fell over. As the struggle continued I looked for an opportunity to handcuff Luke. Corporal Mat held Luke long enough for me to get the handcuffs secured. By this time Luke was swearing at us, spitting and using every bad word in the English language. This was an eye-opener for a new officer. Once Luke was secure in the police car, Corporal Mat turned to me and said, "You were right, I should have said we came to see him and not arrest him." I felt silently proud that I had followed my own instincts about safety and had remembered my training.

Another learning experience for both Corporal Mat and myself involved the arrest of a teenager nicknamed Cricket who was apprehended at his home. Once Cricket was placed in the back of the police car, I asked Corporal Mat why the handcuffs were not put behind the man's back. Corporal Mat indicated, "I know this kid and he would never get out of them." I looked back at the young man who was smiling as he gently tossed the handcuffs to the front seat. Corporal Mat and I looked at each other then at the cuffs lying on the front seat and tried not to laugh.

I attempted not to smile and asked, "How did you do that?"

The reply was simple; "He did not put them tight." I smiled, then asked him, "How did he get the nickname Cricket?"

"My friends call me that because I run so fast and can jump," he added with a sense of pride.

During the first year in Tisdale, I was partnered with Constable Peter, a religious man who, despite his beliefs, did not try to convert me. I felt comfortable working with Peter for two reasons: one, he respected me as a fellow officer and as a woman, and two, he neither flirted with me nor made me feel uncomfortable. He and his wife made Nadine and me feel welcome in their home on many occasions. I felt sad when Peter and his family moved to British Columbia. the following year. As there were only six constables, the partnerships were the same for almost a year.

One of the other officers, Blake, complained he was always working with the same partner and wanted the opportunity to change partners. I had liked working with Constable Peter. I worked occasionally with Blake, Fred, and Frank but not consistently. Blake was a flirtatious officer who made suggestive comments about women and to me. For example, he inquired into my sex life and me being single, whom was I dating, and he boasted that 'he was the man for me'. He would often comment on my body. I suppose he figured that if I worked with him alone and at night, perhaps I may change my attitude and have sex with him. The six officers in the detachment ensured there were always two officers to a shift on the same rotation. Sergeant Chilton decided to change the shift and switch the officers around due to Blake's comments about wanting to have different partners. His reasoning was to allow the junior officers to gain knowledge and experience from the more senior officers, the junior officer in this case being me.

I was to work with Frank, a senior constable with fifteen years experience on the Force. I had no idea that the next shift would change my life forever.

Drunk Partner,
Lies And Deception

ON OUR FIRST NIGHT SHIFT FRANK CAME TO WORK A half-hour late. He and I were to have each taken a ride-a-long student for work experience. I was in the front part of the detachment with the two students. From there I could hear the back door open and close, which meant Frank had arrived. I waited for him to get his gun from his locker and join us in the front office. It seemed a long time for Frank to come down the hall so I asked the students to wait while I walked to the back entrance where the lockers were by the back door. There I saw Frank stagger into his open locker and fall on the floor. I ran to him quickly and noticed he was drunk. He reeked of booze, had red eyes, was falling down and slurred his words. I was angry and scared at the same time. This was our first shift together. I told him to stay by the lockers, I would get our students to wait by the front door in their cars, and then I would drive him home. I knew he needed to sober up and I would have no partner on this night shift. Once I was in the front office the back door slammed. I ran to back, opened the door, only to witness Frank pulling out of the RCMP parking lot in his own car and onto the street. A feeling of panic rose up in my throat as I raced back to the students and told them there was a problem. No sooner had I done that, than there was a knock on the back door. The three of us ran to the back door where a man said he had "just witnessed a police officer hit a parked car, stagger out of the car to a house, get back into the car and drive down the street, swerving". What was I supposed to do? We did not take this in training.

I got into a police car with the two students sitting in the back-seat and drove towards Frank's house. I could not leave the students in the detachment with classified and sensitive documents, nor leave them locked outside. I felt really confused as to what was the right thing to do. I recognized Frank's car swerve onto the street in front of me, roll through a stop sign, nearly miss the turn into his driveway and then he slammed on the brakes to avoid hitting his garage door.

Frank's wife and two daughters came out very upset, and crying. The older daughter said, "Dad was missing mom, he was drinking since lunch." The girls had seen him leave for work and their mom arrived home shortly after. I told his wife to get Frank to bed, hide the car keys, and call if they had any problems. The two ride-a-longs did not get out of the car and therefore were not able to testify as to Frank's intoxication. Lucky me, I could. Later that night, at around two A.M., at the end of my shift, and once the students were gone, Frank came to the office to speak to me. My reaction to him was un-friendly as I was angry that he put me in such a dangerous position.

He asked me about the car he hit so I told him about the wit-ness. He said, "Well, my report will be that the carpet got stuck on the accelerator and that's why I hit the parked car. Right Sherry?" I stared at him in disbelief.

"No Frank, that is not what happened. My report will say, you were drunk and came to work. I will do anything for you, except lie."

He looked so angry and for a second I was frightened.

His response, "Well, I am sending in my report and I know what I need to say."

I went home with a sinking feeling of impending doom. I called an officer who had been transferred from Tisdale several months before, asking for advice on how best to handle this situation. He said, "Take the witness statement, and ask the witness what he thinks was the cause of the accident. Show that statement to Frank and give him the opportunity to change his statement. If Frank won't, tell him that this witness statement is what you are handing in to Sergeant Chilton."

The next day I took a statement from the witness who had observed Frank swerve all over the road, hit the parked car, stagger to the house nearby and knock on the door then stagger back in to his car and drive away. I showed Frank the statement and said, "This is what I am handing in. Perhaps, you need to change your statement!" He refused. He was going to hand in a statement that was a fabrication of the facts.

It was with sadness, trepidation and a heavy heart I handed in the statement to Sergeant Chilton. Needless to say, Chilton was furious that I did not call him. He started to yell at me for not telling him earlier. I explained: "I did not know what to do. A fellow officer coming to work drunk out of his head was not part of our training. This was our first shift working together."

It seemed that I was getting in trouble for Frank's decisions and intoxicated accident. I was the junior member with less than two years of service. To make matters worse, my statement was used by the Crown Counsel to convict Frank of impaired driving. The other officers did not like the fact I had 'turned in' one of their own. It was the beginning of what would be the blue wall of silence.

Frank was to be away for a few weeks at rehab. On the day he left, he called me and thanked me for not lying. He was crying as he explained how he had wanted to stop drinking for years but did not have the courage and that he usually drank when his missed his wife. The RCMP was forgiving to members who admit they have a problem and are willing to go for help.

The atmosphere in the detachment seemed to change overnight. Members would not call me for coffee or talk to me in the office. I began to feel I had done something wrong.

When Frank returned, Sergeant Chilton made us ride as partners. Because of the impaired driving charge, Frank had no license so I was his driver for six months. It was awful because it made the other members have to double up with call outs. They were very angry with me for not covering up Frank's accident and for giving a witness' statement on his intoxication. I was treated like a turncoat. At the start of each shift, the members would go for coffee or something to eat. I would come to work and they would be gone and when I asked to join them, the excuse would be, "We are just finished." I wondered why? Teasing was popular among the detachment staff however, I was called names by two of the members, Blake and Sam which were less than funny. They referred to me as "raisin tits" or "beaver". These comments were made in the office, over the radio and in public, and this name calling was tolerated by our Sergeant. I was embarrassed and asked them to stop. When the comments continued I went to Sergeant Chilton but he did nothing and even suggested I might like the attention. I thought to myself, "what an idiot."

Several months later, December 1991, while at work, I went to use the ladies washroom. As I closed the door in the stall, it fell off the hinges, struck me in the forehead, briefly knocking me out. When I regained consciousness, I staggered to the back door, blood trickling into my eyes, and called my partner, Peter, to return to the detachment and drive me to the hospital. The blow to my head gave me a concussion and I was off work for several days. While being examined at the hospital, I asked Peter to take my gun, use the spare key at work and put the belt in my personal locker. He secured the gun and returned the spare key. The spare keys were only to be used in emergencies such as this to secure our weapons. We had been told by the Sergeant that opening another officer's locker without their permission would not be tolerated.

A few days later when I returned to work, I opened my locker with my key, only to find a dead prairie chicken in my gym bag, blood dripping all over. Someone had opened my personal locker and put in this dead bird. I found this frightening and disgusting. I immediately called Sergeant Chilton. He knew which members would play this kind of joke and "wasn't it funny?" No, it was not funny. One day in January 1992, when I came to work, a plastic hard hat was in my basket. Blake told me it was for washroom doors and falling dead chickens. I did not find this amusing either. I did not know this behaviour was harassment, as the Sergeant never identified it as such. Prior to my arrival there had been other officers who were treated badly by Chilton but they had been transferred to other detachments or quit. I wondered if other female officers were exposed and subjected to this type of ridicule. Looking back, I can see this was most definitely sexual harassment, however, as a young police officer with no support from my superiors, I let things slide for a long time. It was not until I realized the washroom door and chicken incidents were an escalation of violence towards me, I decided to forward a complaint. I made a written submission and complaint to Sergeant Chilton regarding the bathroom door incident, the dead bird episode and addressed the toxic work environment. I forwarded my complaint to Sub Division. The Sergeant had taken no action previously and this resulted in the further alienation by some other officers. Blake and Sam were the jokers and their behaviour was very hurtful.

In retrospect, I can see I was in danger when I answered domestic calls as no one answered my calls for backup. For example, one night I was working with Officer Hal when we received a call regarding a domestic dispute. I recognized the suspect from previous calls as a violent woman hater. I arrived at the scene and requested back up. Hal asked me to confirm the address and get back to him. I insisted this was the right house and I could hear a woman screaming from inside. The ride-a-long, who was sitting beside me was surprised Hal would not back me up. I showed her the radio and how to call for help and, if needed, drive the car away for safety. Suddenly a woman came out of the house screaming, running toward the police car, and following right behind, her violent partner. My heart nearly stopped. I quickly got out of the police car and stepped between the terrified woman and the tall angry man. The pounding in my chest seemed to echo in my ears and I felt as though everything and everyone was in slow motion. My hands were at his chest and I spoke with a deep voice, mostly out of complete fear for my life. All I could think of was the photos I had been shown in training of police officers killed at different domestic disputes. The mistakes made. This was not going to be my fate. I managed to calm the man down to the point where he allowed his wife to get into the police car. From somewhere among the chaos there was a voice, a strong voice, one in control. To my surprise, it was mine. I explained. "I know you are not going to hurt your wife, but sometimes you just get mad. She needs to get some medical help. I know you care about her. Would you let me take her to the hospital and you can see her later? Okay?" I repeated the same words again in a lower voice. "She is hurt and needs help. You want to help her right?"

He slowly began to look more composed and I could see he was calming down. His eyes were glaring but he stopped moving his arms and his shoulders relaxed.

My first priority was the victim, then the suspect, as I only had one car. When I called Hal and told him what happened, he denied he had refused to back me up. I thought to myself, "Lying shit, I have a witness sitting in my car."

The next few months were difficult and a time of alienation. Not only was I looked upon as a traitor for giving a statement on Frank, but it appeared I had no sense of humour. Eventually Sergeant Chilton decided the office should air out the dirty laundry, meaning me. He called a meeting where all the officers of Tisdale Detachment could say what was bothering them. This was not a pleasant experience. Every officer sitting at the table had nothing but bad things to say about me: I had no sense of humour about being called raisin tits" or "beaver"; I could not take jokes regarding the dead bloodied chicken put in my locker; the washroom door incident was a joke; I was not dependable because of what I did to Frank. What really made me angry was Frank saying I needed to build trust again among the other officers. Yet he was the one who came to work drunk and put me in the position where I had to turn him in by giving a statement for the Crown Attorney. It is called honesty and truth, something my badge represents. The other officers looked at me as if I was a 'turncoat' for not protecting Frank. I felt I had done nothing to deserve this reaction. It was a helpless feeling as no one in the room said anything in my defense. Our Sergeant Chilton sat back in his chair and let all the officers, except Peter, say why they did not like or trust me. I cannot recall if Peter had attended this meeting.

Essentially, this toxic work environment was a result of the situation with Frank's drunk driving and the fact I would not lie for him. The meeting was terrible and humiliating. It was unbearable to be in that detachment under these circumstances. For the rest of my service in Tisdale, I had to endure this alienation and harassment. When Peter took an educational leave of absence in the spring of 1992, I was truly alone.

A Dead Man With One Sock

IT IS IMPORTANT TO FOCUS ON THE POSITIVE AND THE Tisdale experience was not all bad. I can recall some of the amusing experiences in which I was involved. One particular call involved a dead man with a single sock.

It was a cold winter morning. A usual Saturday day shift nine A.M. to five P.M. was great because I got to spend the night with Nadine. I arrived at the detachment at nine A.M. just as Hal received a call from the dispatcher. The complainant called in that there could be a problem at one of her rental properties, a seniors' housing complex which consisted of a row of small one or two bedroom bungalows, each self-contained. The tenant was an elderly man about 78 years old with health problems. Upon reaching the home, I saw two sets of footprints, one leading to the large front picture window and one set returning to the road. The footprints going toward the window indicated a slow walk through the deep, heavy snow and it appeared many steps were taken. The other set, however, was like leaps and bounds, just a few very far apart. I was curious and walked to the window.

As I peered in, I saw the tenant lying on the floor, in full view, obviously dead. His hands were stiff and appeared to be reaching in the air, his face staring at me. One can only imagine how the landlady felt when she looked in. Panic!

My partner, Hal, and I entered the home with the landlady behind us. Hal examined the body for signs of foul play while she remained in the kitchen. No marks found to indicate anything suspicious. It was my first thought that he may have died of a heart attack then fallen. The victim was fully dressed except for one sock which was on half his foot. The coffee table had been tipped over and it appeared he had been standing up, attempting to put on his sock and had fallen, hitting the coffee table, then the floor. It was later determined by the doctor he had broken his femur, and with his poor health and age, the loss of blood caused his heart to fail. How many times has this been done?

My partner examined the body and found a wallet in the man's pocket. He asked me for an exhibit bag to secure personal belongings and evidence. I usually kept a couple of these bags in the pocket of my winter coat: it was much easier to have a few bags in my coat than to haul my big briefcase out of the car. I quickly pulled out the bag and something else flew out and landed on the dead man's chest. Hal gasped in surprise. Something was falling in out of the sky onto the body. I looked down and noticed a sanitary pad in its green wrapper had fallen out! I kept a few of those in my pocket as well, in case of emergency. I promptly reached down, picked it up and added, "Well, I don't think he will be needing this." I continued bagging the exhibits with my face flaming red. Hal was polite not to laugh at my embarrassment.

The landlady who made the call was still waiting in the kitchen. She seemed very distressed so I asked if she had been good friends with the deceased. "No, but I was wondering if I needed a lawyer?" She replied.

"Why would you need a lawyer?"

"Because I came here last night looking for the rent money, he was late. He did not answer the door so I walked up to the front window and saw him."

"You saw him last night lying on the floor, looking like that? Perhaps you can let me know why you did not call the police at that time and why did you wait twelve hours?"

"I knew he was dead because he was all stiff looking. I thought I might be in trouble. I just got scared and waited until my husband came home today and talked to him. Am I going to be charged?" I looked at my partner and then said, "There is nothing in the Criminal Code that we can charge you with, so don't worry."

Once she left, Hal added, "Yeah, there is nothing in the Criminal Code to charge someone for being stupid." We both laughed and finished up with the scene. Later that night while getting ready for bed, I thought of the old fellow and how he died. I never put my socks on while standing up.

Another amusing situation occurred when I was working alone on a Sunday night shift, four p.m. to midnight. I was about to drive back to the detachment and close up shop when I noticed the door of Blake's garage was swinging in the wind. He and his family had gone on vacation so I assumed it was a possible break-and-enter in progress. I was the only one on patrol so I went to investigate. The back door was open; all lights were out, the house quiet. I had called for back up from another detachment however, they would only assist after five minutes. I had to access the situation alone and if I failed to respond within that period of time, help would be on the way.

I drew my gun and had my flashlight on but over to the side, in order to confuse anyone who might shoot at me. Hopefully they would shoot towards the light and miss my body. I inched my way in the dark through the garage and up the stairs to a door leading into the house.

I heard a noise and began to follow the sounds. My heart was pounding so hard I thought my chest would explode, my ears were pulsating like a drum, I thought the bad guy would surely hear my bodily functions. I entered the kitchen, scanned the room. Nothing. Silently I entered the living room and looked around. The light bounced back from the TV and pictures on the wall. I walked toward the hallway and turned to check out the three bedrooms. I scanned the hall and suddenly saw a gun pointing back at me from about 10 feet. I dropped to my knees, took cover behind the wall, and focused on what was directly ahead of me, screaming, "POLICE, POLICE!" With my gun pointing dead ahead, my heart stopped beating, and I instantly felt absolutely alone in the dark. I slowly peeked around the corner to confirm the level of danger from the individual looking back. It came as a relief when I realized that it was a mirrored closet at the end of the hallway. I nearly shot a mirror to death! I shook my head in disbelief. The good thing, I did exactly what I was taught, 'always determine the threat and maintain visual contact of any weapon of a suspect.' I checked the remainder of the house and determined all was secure, then locked the back door and got back in the police car to notify dispatch, "All clear." The dispatcher notified me Blake had been located told of the alarm. He had forgotten to lock the back door. I never did tell him that I nearly blew away the hallway mirror!

Work in Tisdale had moments that changed me forever.

What's Wrong With Me?

THE ATTITUDE OF THE OFFICERS CHANGED TOWARD me from the time I had to tell the truth about Frank's drunkenness. I had to watch my back at all times. Every day there were notes on my files commenting on and picking apart every little detail of my actions. For example, 'more time on traffic', 'call the complainant', 'diary dates?' I had to be careful of what I said or did in the detachment and even started to second-guess myself. It was difficult to concentrate on my work.

One evening in September 1992, while having a few drinks at the local pub, I realized I was over the legal limit of .08, and asked a friend sitting at the table if he would drive my car home. He said he only had a couple of drinks so I agreed. There were many cars all exiting the parking lot, each going in different directions at the same time we did. One of our police cars had been waiting on the street with the lights out. They pulled up behind us and activated the police emergency lights so we stopped. My driver said, "Don't worry, I only had a couple, I am fine. There is no way I am over."

One officer, Blake, came to the driver's side, the other, Fred, flashed me in the face with his bright flashlight from passenger side of the car. Fred asked why I wasn't driving.

"Because I have been drinking." I replied.

Blake asked the driver if he had been drinking to which the response was, Yes, probably five all night." Blake asked the driver to come to the police car. I knew he would not be over but within a few minutes, Blake came back to inform me.

"Your driver blew 'over', can you drive the car to the side of the road?"

I said, "No, I've been drinking. I won't take my car, thanks!" Why would a police officer ask someone to drive the vehicle if there is any chance that person had been dinking?

Blake got in the driver's side and drove my car to the shoulder, stopped and got out. Having him in my car beside me made me feel powerless. Fred, Blake and my driver drove away in the police car and then it began to rain.

It had come as a shock when Blake said the driver blew 'over' and they were taking him back to the detachment for a breathalyzer. I got out and stood there in the rain, wondering what my options were. I stood by my car for a few minutes then opened the door on the back passenger's side to get my laundry and walk home. As I did this, the police car came around the corner with the headlights off in the opposite direction, then screeched to a halt beside my car. Blake jumped out and realized I was standing at the back door, not on the driver's side. If I had been in the car on the driver's side, they would have had grounds to charge me, under the Criminal Code, for Care and Control, arrest me, make a breath demand, and force me to submit to a breathalyzer test. I remained silent and realized they had planned to charge me by arresting my driver and leave me with the car, hoping I would be careless or stupid enough to drive home. This was a set-up, thankfully, it backfired on Blake and Fred. I walked home in the pouring rain with laundry basket in tow.

The next day, my friend the driver told me he blew under .08 both times but got a suspension for the night. I began to worry about my safety and spoke to my parents. As a result, I drove Nadine to Gimli to stay with my sister's family while I sorted out my complaint in Tisdale. In forwarding my complaint December 1991, on the discrimination and harassment, I made sure this most recent mistreatment was included.

Should I have been charged with impaired driving, the RCMP would have ample evidence to terminate me. Judging by the manner in which the men at this detachment had been treating me, I was fairly sure any misstep on my part would not be forgiven by the RCMP. It was the beginning of an accurate interpretation of how the RCMP had one set of rules for male officers and a different version of the same rules for women. Looking back, it is obvious of the inequality of treatment between male and female officers.

In October 1991, while working a night shift with Fred Henry and Charles Avani, I observed them wrestling with a local and attempting to handcuff him. The man, who appeared to be in his twenties, was being held over the hood of his car and being handcuffed. I could see the suspect resisting and the two officers were having a difficult time getting this very tall, strong person into the car when I stopped to get out and help. I recognized the young man as Phil who was a good kid except for a foul mouth when he drank. I stood by the officers and said, "Phil, get into the car and don't make matters worse." He immediately stopped struggling against the two arresting officers and allowed Fred to put him in the police car.

Phil looked at me and asked, "Can I talk to you at the detachment?"

"Okay" I replied.

I followed them back to the detachment. When Phil was secured in the breathalyzer room I went to see how he was doing and calm him down. I had a good rapport with the local youth; they trusted me to treat them fairly and honestly. As I approached the room to remind Phil to stay calm and out of trouble, Fred met me in the hallway and flatly refused to let me speak with him.

"We don't need you. You are a distraction."

I could hear Phil calling for me. Fred walked back to the room and told Phil he did not need me. I was upset for Phil as I had said I would talk to him at the detachment. I knew Fred was on one of his power trips. He liked to take a superior attitude and also enjoyed watching people suffer the embarrassment of being in custody. The next day, I did speak with Phil and explained what had happened. He admitted he had given the officers a hard time. However, these egotistical "little boys" let their pride get in the way of acknowledging I might be able to handle people in a more positive manner. Working with the public, both victims and offenders gave me the greatest fulfillment.

There was one incident, however, where, even though I could have helped resolve a problem, my Sergeant told me not to get involved in another officers' business. I had no idea he would order me to break the law and not help a child who had been kidnapped by one of our own officers.

Kidnapped And Helpless

ONE SHIFT DURING MY TWO YEARS AT TISDALE detachment, I was again working alone on a Saturday day shift. It was springtime and the weather warm with sweet smells of fresh cut grass and rain. I had sent my daughter, Nadine, to be with my family in Gimli, Manitoba, while I sorted out the intolerable situation at work. While sitting in the detachment working on files, I received a frantic phone call on the office administration line from Blake's common-law wife, Mary, who was upset and crying so hard I could hardly understand what she was saying. She was gasping for breath as she spoke, her voice shaky. I was aware she and Blake were having relationship problems and they had a separation agreement. Apparently, she had full custody of their two-year-old daughter, Lisa, and Blake had visitation rights. Blake was to have brought Lisa home the day before but had not done so. He told Mary he was not bringing Lisa back and was heading out to his brother Jeff's place in Beaver Narrows. Blake's older brother, Jeff, was also an RCMP officer. Mary was frantic.

She further explained the custody order clearly stated she had full custody of Lisa with Blake having visitation rights.

I asked her about the visitation time frame and various stipulations set out on the order, what time Blake was to pick up and return Lisa, and if he was allowed to take her out of town without Mary's consent. She said she called me because she knew I would do something to help her, and the other officers would not. I advised her I did not have much experience in this area and would call my supervisor, Sergeant Chilton, for suggestions as to what to do. I could identify with her panic in not being able to locate her child. A mother's worst fear is to lose her child.

I was completely shocked by Chilton's response to this complaint. He advised me, "to stay out of Blake's business, things will sort themselves out."

I was not sure if I had heard him correctly and again told him of the situation and the custody order. "Blake was breaking the law!"

His voiced seemed angry and again told me to "stay out their personal affairs and this is an order." He slammed the phone down and I was left holding the receiver in a state of shock and stunned silence. I had just been ordered to break the law. In training we were instructed if a situation came up where an order was given to break a law, as a police officer, we had the right to refuse the unlawful order, and the RCMP would protect us from prosecution and retribution from within.

I phoned Mary back and told her what had transpired. I felt so helpless as a police officer and I wondered whom I could call to help in this situation. From her reaction I think she had half expected this response. Something inside me said 'call a lawyer from town and let him know what is happening and get his advice on what Mary can do and her rights.' I told Mary what I was thinking, that I would call an attorney in town with whom I was familiar, relay the entire situation, get his opinion on what she should do, and what I should do.

Needless to say the attorney was stunned as I informed him of the situation and the order I got from Chilton. He advised I had 'done the right thing' in calling him. Now documented from outside the force, the legal ramifications were immense. If Blake had harmed the child, I could have been held responsible and, given the present work environment in Tisdale, possibly charged under the Criminal Code and the RCMP Act. I knew I could trust this attorney as I had previous dealings with him in court for traffic tickets. In court he was respectful to the police and dedicated to his clients.

Mary was pleased with what I had done and called back after she had spoken with the attorney. An hour later, I was working on my files when I heard the back door slammed. My supervisor, Sergeant Chilton came into the office, looking extremely agitated. I was so angry with him I could barely speak or look at his cowardly face. He had failed to support me with the name calling and the situation with drunken Frank. I suffered because of his lack of leadership and integrity.

When he asked about Mary and my telephone call I simply responded, without looking at him, "I called a lawyer and advised him of the situation and what you told me to do. Then I called Mary and relayed information that the lawyer would be getting in touch with her and would handle it, possibly through another detachment."

I was frightened about telling him what I had done but knew I was right. I had to protect the child as well as myself. Sergeant Chilton started yelling at me for going over his head. My jaw was tight as I explained, "Blake was breaking the law, you told me to do nothing and stay out of it. It was not our business."

My heart was pounding so hard in my chest. I thought it was going to explode. Sergeant Chilton is a big man with a scary stern face. He also has a terrible temper. The intimidation factor of the difference in rank was terrifying. He was several ranks above me. I just stood there with a blank look on my face and, at that moment, I think he realized he had made a big mistake. Not only was the order illegal, but the little girl, Lisa, could have been in danger. Even the most rational person can behave in an irrational and dangerous manner when emotions are high. Sergeant Chilton went back to his office for a few minutes, then came out and left without saying a word to me. I called the lawyer and Mary to let them both know what had transpired. This is called 'protecting yourself.' Later in the day, Mary called back to let me know Blake was bringing Lisa back that evening and he was sorry. I guess he realized if he did not obey the custody order, he could be charged and possibly fired from the RCMP. Blake and Mary got back together but my friendship with Mary was strained. However, she knew as a police officer, I would be willing to help her again.

Trip To The Shrink

THE HARASSMENT INCREASED AND MY FELLOW OFFICERS made me feel I could do nothing right. I was questioned about the tickets I wrote; I was called at home as to a location of one of my files that could not be found with the implication I had taken the file home. By trying to show I was not bothered about this change in attitude towards me seemed to make it worse. As a result, I contacted the Inspector in charge of Prince Albert Sub Division, of which Tisdale is a detachment. I was requesting a transfer due to problems. He did not validate my concerns nor show any interest in solving the problem. I explained the name-calling and sexual harassment, the dead chicken incident, the washroom door falling on my head, and the alienation from the officers for giving a statement against Frank on the impaired driving charge. He sent a response, which indicated it was me who had the problem communicating with people. The letter also stated I was not willing to accept an apology for the 'joke' with the dead chicken being placed in my private gun locker.' He could find no evidence an officer was to blame for the incident of the washroom door that fell and gave me a concussion. Therefore, he found my complaint of harassment invalid and I would not be transferred. All the unrelenting and sadistic harassment was simply dismissed, I was viewed as the problem and I had to learn to live with it. He also recommended I should see a psychologist to learn how to get along with others.

This recommendation shook my self-concept as to who I was and what my life meant. How could I be so wrong? What did I need to do? I had no idea. These doubts began to make me question my everyday life. I had always thought I had a good sense of humour and got along with most people. During April 1992, a couple of weeks after receiving the letter, an appointment was made for me to see Dr. Reader, the RCMP psychologist. If the RCMP wanted to get rid of me they needed evidence to substantiate I was poisoning the work environment, and unwilling to improve myself. I felt intimidated at going to see a psychologist, but believed and hoped by telling the truth about what was happening in Tisdale, perhaps he could help.

At our first meeting, I explained my family situation as a single mother, and the work environment. I described in detail the series of events that had lead to the current situation, the lack of support, and how I had tried to talk to the officers, and the further alienation I was feeling. He listened and asked questions for clarification.

About an hour into the meeting, he advised me, "Sherry, I can see just by talking to you today that you don't have a problem in communicating and getting along with people. The RCMP will not transfer you but I can send you to a therapist who will help you develop the skills you're going to need to survive in Tisdale." He suggested a therapist could give me the added coping skills I would need to continue to work and maintain a career. He recommended a therapist in Saskatoon, as other officers who had met with her received positive results. Dr. Reader is a mental health professional employed by the RCMP. It was vindication for me, and gratifying that he suggested I learn to survive illegal situations and cope with sexual harassment within the

RCMP organization. First, I had to learn about myself.

In the summer of 1992, I met with a wonderful red-haired woman, who, I can honestly say, has saved my life on several occasions by bringing me back from what, at times, seemed to be the threshold of the black abyss of hopelessness. She taught me how to cope with the abuse and I learned to accept myself. Most of my life growing up in a large family I had to learn skills to survive. With older and younger siblings I found that if I was really nice all the time, I stayed out of trouble. However, in communicating anger or negative feelings I did have a difficult time. With the therapist's help I learned effective coping skills and improved communication of negative feelings. My therapist helped me to realize I have a right to feel my feelings. I have the right to say "no," and to accept that some problems may be my responsibility. Learning about the dynamics and inner workings of me was difficult, and changing a behavior pattern was even more difficult. I began to be more aware of old patterns and the negative effect they had on me, Nadine, my family, myself and the work environment. I learned more effective communication skills which enabled me to express my dislike for a situation or comments. Prior to therapy, I was afraid to speak up. With my therapist's guidance, l became aware the problems in Tisdale had nothing to do with my communication style, but with the male officer's attitude towards women. I accepted the officers at Tisdale Detachment were not going to change, so I had to learn better techniques in how to communicate, and how to respond to their behaviour.

At my first meeting with the therapist in Saskatoon I felt nervous because I thought, 'this is silly going to a therapist to learn to cope'. I was under the illusion I knew all the coping skills necessary for life. How naive and wrong I was. My therapist opened me up and peeled back the layers of pain and disappointment, like one would the skins of an onion. By the end of the third session, I looked forward to the next week, although I was unaware of how difficult competent and intensive true psychotherapy can become, and how traumatic it is to look at yourself without blaming others.

All my life I was able to keep my emotions stuffed deep inside which I thought was people did as adults. At the fourth meeting, the therapist cracked me open like an egg. The question that opened my inner feelings was regarding my love for Nadine and her future. I cried and cried. I admitted my current work situation was difficult, as well as being tired and cranky all the time, made me feel useless as a mother, which was not the reason I joined the RCMP. I joined to get off welfare, to be able to support her and give her wonderful opportunities. That was my first step in the understanding and forgiving of others and myself.

On subsequent visits, I began to learn how to take complete responsibility for my actions, the choices I had made, and the consequences which followed. This was very difficult. I had to admit to myself that I am vulnerable when I drink too much, so I needed to learn my limits. I did not have to be flirtatious nor respond to flirtations from male officers in order to be liked or valued. She also made it easier to begin to allow myself to be angry. All my adult life I had repressed my anger in certain aspects of relationships. As a child, when I showed anger or rebellion, I would be disciplined. There were so many kids, not enough money, and adults who were not able to exhibit healthy communication techniques. I also had to admit I did not have a perfect family and had observed most families behave in similar fashion to my own home life. Looking back, I can see there were some of dysfunctions due to parents who were not always able to meet the individual needs of seven children. My mother was busy with raising the kids, which left her little or no time for herself, and in retrospect, my father thought only of his work. He enjoyed sports and participated in that part of our lives, but was not the active parent needed for seven children. I was able understand the importance of releasing anger and pain from the past. Otherwise, this repressed pain builds up a lifetime of hurt and anger and can come out directed elsewhere, sometimes, at the innocent. Over the years this pain turns into bitterness and resentment. Forgiveness takes time. Accepting our mistakes frees us to move forward in life. It was important to me to understand we all make mistakes, given the situation and life skills we have learned.

Over the years, I realized relationships need compassion, forgiveness and without mistakes there is no growth. As a parent I would probably make mistakes with my daughter. It took some time, but I did learn to accept the relationship I have with both my parents. I accept their flaws and love each parent in my own way. There are no perfect people and I am reminded we all struggle in life as challenges are placed in our path. Every relationship takes effort, and I have worked at understanding my family, loving them for what they are to me today. I hope people can accept and love me in spite of all my flaws. However, forgiving and acceptance took time.

I was not used to letting out my anger and yet, with the help of the therapist, learned skills that helped prevent my keeping the pain inside. At first, I thought some of these tools were too bizarre. For example, I learned to use a paper bat and kneel on the floor in my bedroom, bang the bat against the bed and scream in a deep voice what was bothering me. I made sure not to do this when Nadine was in the house as I was afraid she would be upset hearing me scream.

By allowing myself to let go of past or present anger and dealing with pain, I was able to comprehend my own feelings. I looked at myself and my life with different eyes, moving towards a more understanding and forgiving sense of being. I continue to work on this aspect to this day. I believe this is a lifelong experience. I was able to recognize the victim role I was in and became a stronger player in this game of life where I was responsible for myself and my actions. Knowing what I wanted, needed and was entitled to was half the battle. Improving communication was the next step.

With continued therapy, I put into practice the coping skills. My therapist taught me how to use clear language and the 'I' messages which helped me to better communicate with the officers in Tisdale. Using the word 'I' when communicating helps lessen the likelihood of the other person becoming defensive. For example, when I spoke to Blake about his name calling, I would say "Blake, when you call me those names I feel humiliated and cheap, would you please stop?"

This took lots of practice and courage. At first I was scared every time I felt it necessary to use this 'new language'. As a child I had never learned to communicate effectively, so this was absolutely foreign to me. My therapist was completely supportive as I struggled in my self-awareness and in learning new coping skills. I was not always happy with her questions, such as, "What are you feeling as you say that?" Or, "Why do you deserve that treatment?" Or. "How are you feeling?" These questions probed into my soul, and later I realized this had to be done in order to move ahead with life.

Throughout our six months of weekly visits, I learned to better understand myself, accept my choices in life, my family and the Tisdale officers. I also was able to recognize the harassment would not stop with therapy so, in order to maintain a successful career in the RCMP, steps had to be taken by me to get a transfer. Through therapy, I gained the emotional strength to forward a complaint to the Canadian Human Rights Commission, an agency outside the RCMP. This was an important and courageous step and it took a long time to decide to follow through with the complaint. I had to weigh the pros and cons of forwarding a letter of complaint and the possible ramifications from the Tisdale officers. My courage and resolve were about to be tested in ways I could not yet comprehend.

My complaint to Sub Division had not been acted upon and I did not know what my options were. The officers at Tisdale thought I had tried to make them look bad in the eyes of Sub Division. In February 1992 a RCMP friend had warned me as the Sub Division Inspector had not supported my claim of harassment, Sergeant Chilton would make my life hell. My friend was deadly accurate. The situation went from bad to worse.

I spoke to Sergeant Chilton who addressed the issues of name-calling and other 'jokes' with Blake and Sam. In April 1992, Sam did my yearly evaluation. One can only imagine how objective and fair his judgment would be in doing my assessment. His report stated I had no common sense, was immature and not trustworthy. It seemed all my files were being handed back to me with comments such as 'poor work' or 'not good enough.' The idea was to pick apart everything I did to make it appear I was unfit to be a member of the RCMP and thus accumulate the ammunition to fire me. Under such constant scrutiny, it is impossible for anyone to look competent. Essentially, according to the assessment of me, I was not capable of performing at even a minimal level of competence.

It appears I was not the only female in Tisdale Detachment to have difficulties with the management style of the detachment commander. Prior to my arrival in 1990, there had been four officers and two secretaries who had resigned at the detachment under the leadership of Sergeant Chilton. To my mind, Tisdale had become dangerous emotionally and physically. One evening after my first year in Tisdale, I had been followed home from the local bar. Upon entering my home I kept the lights still off and I peered outside. I observed a police car pull into my driveway, then back out and drive away several times. I lived on the outskirts of town with an elderly landlady who lived in the basement. She had not called the police, so why were they in the driveway? This was one of many incidents that began as little comments and escalated to my physical and mental well-being. Some officers felt I had no sense of humour or could not take a joke. For example, when the washroom door at work had fallen on my face because the hinges had been removed. Blake could not understand why I did not find that funny. Blake admitted to going into my gun locker to put the bloodied dead chicken in the gym bag. I received calls at home from officers criticizing me for work I had done. I was worried about losing my job and I was scared! If I had been attacked or felt threatened, who from the RCMP would have helped me?

While Nadine was in Gimli, I contemplated my next move. Would the next step be resigning from the RCMP? What about my financial future? Sergeant Chilton was incompetent as a leader, he failed to stop the name-calling, failed to stop the harassment and he failed to encourage a friendly work environment. He laughed with the officers regarding the washroom door and chicken incidents. He failed to show any public support for me, and although privately he supported my concerns, at the office he went along with Blake and Sam and their jokes. He wanted his promotion, and was not going to let anything stand in the way of having a spotless record of a harassment free detachment.

I met with Inspector Strait of Prince Albert Sub Division, who was next in the chain of command from my sergeant. He suggested that 'things would be better if I did not make a formal complaint and no negative baggage would follow me.' Essentially he was warning me that the officers of Tisdale detachment would never work with me if I sent forward a formal complain of harassment. I wondered, "What were my options? Do nothing and have the situation continue or make a complaint and have it stopped?" I considered doing nothing, but the end result would be, I felt, a nervous breakdown for me. If I made the complaint, the officers would further alienate me. In addition, this complaint would follow me to my next detachment. Thinking about the possible worse case scenarios was exhausting and in the end, decided sending the complaint could give me a much needed new start. I chose to send the complaint.

The negative comments, blatant disregard for me and alienation by the officers at Tisdale detachment were apparent to officers from other detachments. Officers who traveled through our detachment often came for coffee and they noticed some of the officers at Tisdale detachment would not even acknowledge that I was at the table, and made faces when I spoke. I saw the shocked look on their faces regarding the manner in which I was being treated, and these guests asked me later in private what was going on at work? What could I say? I had to work here.

One evening shift in chilly February 1992, I could not open the back or front doors to the detachment. I pounded on the back door but no one appeared to be inside. Then I waited for maybe fifteen minutes for the rest of the shift to arrive. A police car pulled up in the back parking lot where I was standing in the freezing cold. An officer was bringing in a prisoner so I told him about the problem of the locked doors. I used his car radio to call the dispatch center and asked them to notify the other officers on shift to attend the detachment for the prisoner. Suddenly the back door opened and Blake appeared. He said he not heard me at the door. I looked at the officer escorting the prisoner and he said, "Is this against you?" I shrugged. I went to my basket and found the new key to the office. I had not been notified the locks had been changed nor why.

The atmosphere had certainly deteriorated from the time I first arrived in February of 1990. At that time I had been admired by the other officers for my performance in police duties. I recall one incident that was especially gratifying.

One evening in the fall of 1990, Hal and I were called to a fight in progress on the street. As our police car pulled up to the scene I could see a huge man pounding the life out of someone on the ground. Hal was the driver and as a passenger could observe the fight in progress. We pulled up and stopped, but Hal got out of the car too slowly from my perspective: all I could see was the poor fellow on the ground trying to use his arms to defend and protect his head. I ran across the road and jumped on the back of the big fellow; put him in a chokehold wrapping my legs around his waist to keep my grip. He struggled against me as I held on tightly. Within a coupe of seconds, he fell over backward from loss of consciousness. The combined weight was heavy and I could feel my body slammed into the pavement with a thud. He was on top of me with my legs still wrapped around his body I had the man subdued.

By the time Hal got to us, I had relaxed my arms and struggled to maintain a hold of his limp body. It was easy to put the cuffs on him. The victim was surprised as he got up slowly to see in his words was a 'wee slip of a girl', who took down the big brute. I was winded as we fell hard onto the road but the adrenalin had kicked in and I did not let go until the cuffs were on. It was only a matter of seconds from start to finish. The suspect regained consciousness as soon as I let go of the chokehold. He was staggering as he got to his feet and swearing. "Fucking cops, who the fuck did this. Man, I won't forget this. Fucking shit." I do not think he realized that I was a female officer. First of all, he had been drinking and second, the uniform is hardly flattering! It makes female officers look bulky. Even the slim female officers end up looking shapeless and chunky. Looking fashionably cute in my uniform was never a concern.

We managed to get him into the police car and back to the detachment. The suspect was angry and began yelling and making threats against the officer who jumped on him. He thought Hal had been the officer who took him down. Hal said "No, it was my partner, do you want to see her?" The suspect was surprised, "Her?" He did not believe him.

Hal called for me to come to the cell area. The man was about 6'4" and over 220 pounds. I was 5'6" and about 130 pounds. The suspect looked at me in utter dismay and shock. I just smiled my sweetest smile and said, "Hi". He kept staring then turned to sit on the bed, embarrassed that it had been a girl, not a big hulking male officer, who had taken him out. I walked back to the front office to finish my paperwork.

During the remainder of my time in Tisdale, I would see this big fellow but he never bothered me. It was a short 'hi' when we met in the streets. Nor did he ever tell his friends a female officer arrested him. The positive response from the other officers regarding this incident was, however, short lived.

SHERRY LEE BENSON-PODOLCHUK

No Understanding,
No Forgiveness

I WAS THE ONLY FEMALE AT TISDALE DETACHMENT AND, after my first year, began to think about other female officers and their experiences. Out of curiosity, I prepared a questionnaire on the work environment, relationships between male and female officers, stress of shift work and family life and other possible conflicts. In March, I sent this out to several female officers in the sub division. This was strictly for my own interest. I had no idea that people would take an innocent inquiry as an attack on the Tisdale detachment.

After I had sent out the questionnaire, I went on holidays for a week and on my return, while driving home with my small child, I observed a car in front of me swerving all over the road. I thought, "a possible impaired driver." This was just a few miles outside Tisdale. The driver was hitting the shoulder then over the centre line, speeding up, slowing down and then, without warning, he slowed to a stop. I pulled up behind him as though I was in a police vehicle and approached the driver. The lone occupant was drunk, hunched over the wheel and almost asleep, the inside of the car reeked of booze.

I identified myself as an officer of RCMP Tisdale and advised him he was under arrest for impaired driving. I made a mental note of the time. The traffic was heavy and I was concerned he would kill someone and I helped him into the back seat of my private vehicle. His intoxication made him very submissive and he was only too happy to get a ride. Another car stopped to see what was going on so I identified my self as an off-duty RCMP officer and the man offered to help. I asked him to call the Tisdale Detachment, explain that Constable Benson was bringing in an impaired driver in her private vehicle, her small child was with her and please send back up. I waited a few minutes but no one came. Nadine was tired and didn't like the 'stinky man', sleeping in the back seat, so I drove to the detachment. In hindsight, I realize this was not a wise decision for the safety of Nadine and myself. Upon my arrival, I was feeling pleased with having taken an impaired driver off the road, but at the same time disappointed with no one coming out to pick up the man. I quickly noticed the atmosphere was less than receptive at the detachment. Blake, Fred and Dennis were all there. I put the drunk in the breathalyzer room and waited for one of them to do the test. The test takes about 40 minutes so this is when I took Nadine home to the babysitter. She was tired and wanted to have a bath. I told her I would be home before bed. Back at the detachment, the mood had not improved. Blake and Fred would not even look at me. I thought 'what the hell is going on?' After the processing and securing the drunk in the cells, I left for the night.

The next day shift was the same. Sergeant Chilton and Sam did not acknowledge I was back from holidays nor that I had arrested a drunk driver the previous night. Peter was working with me and asked if I noticed the change in the atmosphere with the fellows. I said, "Yes I did," and inquired, "What is going on?" He told me one of the female officers who received the questionnaire took it to her boss, who then called my boss, Sergeant Chilton, who promptly had a fit. I have been in the same building when he has had one of these temper tantrums and it is scary. He does not seem to care about respect, privacy or confidentiality when dealing with the officers. Normally when something like this happens, one would like to believe the supervisor would remain calm, gather facts before making outrageous statements, such as implying I wanted to destroy his leadership and every officer was terrible to work with. Peter told me Chilton was swearing when he got the call and the entire office was privy to his outrage. He had not bothered to wait until my return from holidays to inquire about my motives in sending the questionnaire and the result was the whole situation blown out of proportion. Also, as I had been working at the Tisdale Detachment for over a year, I thought my honesty would have been accepted by the other officers. How wrong I was. These officers chose not to ask about my motives and simply believed I was out to 'get them'. It was also disappointing no one made any attempt to take the time to contact me to inquire about my possible motives and concerns. Usually in police work, it is important to first gather the facts and not let assumptions cloud the truth.

I had no idea what the problem was until Peter told me the reaction the other officers had to the questionnaire. They had felt betrayed. I wanted to mend this rift as quickly as possible so I went to each officer individually and explained the questionnaire was no reflection on the detachment, I was merely inquiring if other female officers, both single and married, had babysitting problems and other issues unique to women. I also asked about how female officers fit in with male officers. I apologized for the misunderstanding. However, I received the same uncooperative response from each of them. They thought the questionnaire was a reflection on the Tisdale Detachment and other detachments would think Tisdale is a lousy place to work. My response to their interpretation was, "Well, if I sent out a questionnaire on hemorrhoids, would you think I was saying that all officers in Tisdale detachment had hemorrhoids?" My explanation shrugged off. Chilton did say had I been a man, the fellows would have forgiven me.

I did not realize at the time the real harassment was about to begin, and this was the beginning of the end. I could not believe they were such chauvinistic 'little boys'.

It seemed on every shift from April 1991 to December 1992, I received the cold shoulder. I was not asked to go for coffee. Blake, Sam, Hal or Fred, would go for lunch but did not tell or invite me to join them, nor would they drive in my police car during a night shift. While doing paper work in the office, they would not speak to me at all. Peter was my saving grace. He accepted my explanation as the truth because he could see I had integrity and would not be deliberately hurtful. I think his religious beliefs also enabled him not to be so judgmental. He said he and his wife had prayed for things in the office to improve and he offered explanations as to the negative feelings the other officers may have towards female officers. Peter was the only one who did not complain when I did not spend more time after shift completing paperwork.

My response was, "I don't have a wife." Mainly, as a single mom with a small child, I did the same work as their wives plus a police job. Blake and Fred were gossips and would ask Peter whom I was fucking, if anyone. Of course he relayed his disgust to their question. The fact I rejected their sexual invitations or requests for a date must have made them frustrated. I tried to keep my private life just that, private. I had made the mistake of going to detachment parties, where after a few drinks, some of the fellows thought it was okay to flirt and touch me. At first, I enjoyed the attention and wanted to belong. However, once I went for therapy, I did not attend many parties as I realized this behaviour was affecting how I was respected as an officer.

I do not think Blake and Sam liked the fact I wanted the groping to stop. They were both married, yet they continued the behaviour and the message was not getting through to them that 'No' is 'No'. It was a combination of several issues that made the rift among Blake, Fred and me even wider. The cumulative effect of my sending out the questionnaire, addressing the issue of name-calling, requesting, "please keep their filthy hands off me," and my statement about Frank's impaired driving, probably destroyed any chance of acceptance and respect from these men.

Blake, Fred and Sam would not talk to me during our shifts. Peter informed me they would go through my workbasket and pick apart everything I had done, fundamentally making fun of me and referring to me as 'Bimbo'. It was mob mentality. Peter kept his opinion to himself and did not join in because it was not his nature. He was a forgiving and understanding man. I was sad to see him take his educational leave and return with his family to Vancouver. Then I was truly alone in this hellhole of a detachment. In the back of my mind, a twinge of fear began to grow. In training, we did not learn what steps to take when being harassed and abused by the officers of your own detachment. To whom could I turn? I was rejected by the officers of the RCMP: how could I ever expect them to help in a time of crisis? I had no idea I would very shortly be a victim with no one I could call on for help.

How Could This Happen To Me,
A Police Officer?

WHILE I WAS IN TISDALE, I SELDOM WENT OUT, OR TO the local bar. It was easier for the male officers to go drinking and not have their reputations tarnished but in my case the townspeople complained to my boss that, as a single mother, I had a reputation to uphold. Some woman had called the office to complain I was wearing a mini dress and it was 'unprofessional'. My Supervisor called me into the office to talk to me. I was wearing the dress and he just said, "nice flowers" and let me know of the complaint. My dress was short and figure forming, with flowers of various shades of purple. I said I would wear whatever I want on my own time. He agreed and that was that.

One evening, later in the spring of 1992, I had gone out with a few friends, had too much to drink, and was feeling free of stress. A man kept bugging me to go home with him. He was sitting beside me and put his hand on my thigh. I wasn't interested and pushed his hand away. He was a touchy-feely kind of pest. Then he left the table and my friends and I kept partying. I did not know that he followed me home and waited outside my house while the babysitter left. My babysitter later confirmed she saw him outside but thought I knew about it. I went to bed feeling overpowered with the need to sleep. I was completely unaware the man had come into my house, into my bedroom and was waiting for me in the dark.

I woke up in the dark to the feeling my overalls being pulled off my legs. In my alcohol-induced state I tried to focus on what was going on and what could I do. There were hands moving up my legs from the end of the bed, tugging at my underwear. I could sense fingernails dig into my skin as my underwear was pulled down. The black figure at the foot of my bed seemed to engulf me. I felt powerless. My mind quickly focused and I could see a dark figure standing at the foot of my bed. I was scared sober but could not move. The figure moved to the opposite side of the bed and as he passed by the window, the yard light shone on part of his face. I became frightened. What would I do if I screamed and Nadine woke up? What would he do to her? What about the elderly landlady downstairs, would he hurt her? I blamed myself for drinking and letting this happen. I kept deathly quiet and waited for the end. I wished I had taken my gun home, at least I might have threatened him to get out. Should I scream or not scream? What do you do when a man breaks into your bedroom in the middle of the night? I felt my brain go empty of ideas.

I could sense him getting closer to me on the bed and felt sick to my stomach. My eyes remained shut and I pretended to be asleep. He was big, not but strong. The pressure of his body forced the air out my lungs. I felt the pressure of his legs as he maneuvered between my thighs. 'Yuck' was all I was thinking. The odour of his breath added to the nauseating sensation growing in my throat. He must have been drunk because he penetrated me but rolled off after a minute. It seemed longer. I wanted to fuse my legs together forever. He pulled me close so that I was forced to be touching the entire side of his body; I remained completely motionless, trying desperately not to let my breathing stir him. He started to snore. I lay there terrified for several hours until the light of day filled my room and I heard the birds outside singing their sweet songs. No one was aware of the horror I was experiencing. The helplessness. A cop without her gun is useless. I wished I had my gun, but I left it at work to make sure Nadine never had an opportunity to get hurt. My body ached from being tense for hours. I desperately needed a Javex bleach bath to clean myself. I moved my head slowly in an attempt to see if it was safe to move, but my slight movement caused him to stir and wake up.

I closed my eyes and again I pretended to be asleep. His breath was even more foul as he pulled me under him and raped me again. How could he do this to me, a cop? I am supposed to defend people and I can't defend myself or stop this horrible act. I felt so powerless. The only thought racing around in my head was "please God! Don't let Nadine wake up." My prayers were answered: she slept late. The second attack seemed to last forever: for this time he was forceful and aggressive as he was shoving himself into me. He stunk of last night's booze and cigarette breath. I ached inside. With each thrust, I was ripped apart, my body stiff as a corpse. In my mind I was not there but watching from outside my body at this horror. He swore when he could not finish the job and flopped onto my chest. The weight made it difficult to remain motionless as his breathing was hard and pushing on my chest as I tried to breath. It seemed like forever before he got off me. I had my head turned away, but I could see through one squinted eye he was getting dressed.

Suddenly I found my courage, from somewhere inside me I will never know. I grabbed at the blanket at my feet to cover up body. I could not think of anything to say, I could not even look at him. I felt so dirty with disgust and hate. I just wanted to clean every inch of my body. He watched me get up and said something to effect that I had a 'nice ass.' I nearly vomited on the floor by his feet. I held my breath in fear as I moved passed him out of the bedroom, terrified that he would hurt me. I noticed Nadine's bedroom door was closed as I raced to bathroom and I turned on the bath water. Listening at the door for any sounds, I waited to hear the sound of the front door closing. He was gone. Thank God! Yuck! I looked at the reflection in the bathroom mirror. Starring back was a different face, the eyes filled with fear, nausea overwhelming, a sense of disgust, shock, and shame. The deepest dread made me realize the face was mine. Thinking about this makes me want to vomit again.

I have only spoken about this event with my therapist and a friend. However, once I was in therapy, slowly, I was able to deal with the pain and accept what had happened to me, and realized it was not my fault. I still do not know how I was able to function in those days and months that followed the attack. I must have just blocked it out. I could not count on the Tisdale detachment to help at work so why would they give me any support if I were to report I was raped and brutalized by a stranger. I kept this horror quiet, went to work, and played with my daughter. This shame clung to me for years, sitting in my soul making me feel unclean and left with little self-esteem. From my perspective, this violation was like having part of my personality that is fun and free, ripped away. It was many years before I was able to take my power back.

From Bad To Worse

EVENTUALLY I GOT ASSIGNED THE 'SHIT JOBS' IN THE detachment. Sergeant Chilton and Corporal Jones were both super-visors and as such could assign files to anyone they choose. One job, which all officers disliked, was the duty of informing family members of a death. In training we were shown the policy and procedure in de-livering this type of news and possible reactions. One night shift dur-ing the winter, a call came in from the dispatcher who had received a message from the United States regarding the death of a relative of a local resident. Notification had to be done at once so Sam assigned me to do the job immediately upon my arrival at the detachment for my shift.

I called the family residence and was told by the babysitter the entire family was at a wedding social at the local recreation centre. As I approached the centre, I could feel dread building up inside me. The music was booming, sounds of laughter and cheers to good health could be heard as I entered the doorway to the party. A man came up to me and asked "What is the problem officer?" I said "Good evening sir, there is no problem, I would like to talk to Mrs. -------." He left to go and get her. As she approached the feeling of dread began to build again and I was on edge, waiting for an emotional outburst.

She walked up to me smiling. Her smile began to fade as she looked at my serious face. As the music was loud, I gently pulled her aside so that I would not have to yell the news. "Mrs.------, I am very sorry to inform you that your uncle Mr. ---- has died. The news came to our detachment and we were asked to notify you immediately, I am so sorry." Before I had the last two words out of my mouth, she threw herself into my arms, and said, "Thank God, this is great, he has been in such pain. This is a blessing. Thank you so very much!" I was in complete shock. This was not the reaction I had been expecting! We spoke for a few of minutes about her uncle, then other relatives came to see what the commotion was about. Here I was hugging the woman and a mob of people coming toward me. When she told them the news, it was the same reaction, one of relief. I was invited to come in for a drink and something to eat. I thanked them for offer but advised as I was on duty I would have to leave. She again thanked me for bringing her the good news. I left the building with a strange feeling inside. I felt no matter what happens at the detachment level, I will not let it affect the manner in which I deal with the public.

The toxic environment at the detachment continued and summer into late fall of 1992, I began to fear for my health. I had stomach problems, constipation and/or diarrhea, headaches and anxiety. I had trouble sleeping and getting the mental rest required for my job as a police officer. I went to see my physician several times and explained details of the events and how the stress at work was affecting me. She prescribed a mild sleeping pill to help me get an undisturbed sleep. However, I found I could sleep with the medication but was unable to hear Nadine if she called in the night, so I did not take them as regularly as prescribed. Mentally I tossed around the idea of proceeding with a harassment complaint and the possible ramifications. I knew the RCMP was unforgiving and the officers in Tisdale would continue to make my life a living hell. Finally I decided that I would send Nadine back to Gimli and forward the complaint. Once Nadine was out of harm's way, I could concentrate on protecting myself. I decided to fight back and move ahead with the Canadian Human Rights Commission. I also decided to resign, as I could no longer deal with the situation.

One can imagine the reaction to news of the complaint and the reason I was finally transferred out of Tisdale Detachment. What I found to be frustrating was the fact that Sergeant Chilton was promoted in the summer of 1992 and moved to a new detachment.

By December 1992, my formal complaint to the Canadian Human Rights appeared to be settled to the satisfaction of all. However, I cannot discuss the settlement as long as I am employed with the RCMP. My complaint was against two of the officers at Tisdale detachment for sexual harassment. I had no choice but to defend myself. The RCMP was setting me up by giving me a poor performance assessment and putting me on the Reporting System. Once I was on the Reporting System everything I did at work was scrutinized under a microscope for mistakes. It was a horrible experience. Self-doubt creeps into your soul. The organization that I was so proud to represent was trying to fire me for protecting myself against sexual harassment.

The incoming Sergeant, Hank, was forced to deal with the terrible morale problem at the detachment. Perhaps had he arrived earlier, things might have been different but by the fall of 1992, it was too late.

He asked me, "Why did you send in the complaint?" I told him, "The RCMP was not listening to me and nothing was being done to stop the harassment. You are the medicine that arrived too late to save this toxic detachment." Hank noted, "Well, they are listening to you now."

By now, the situation at the detachment had become entrenched with little chance of resolution. The RCMP was not accustomed to officers challenging harassing behaviour. The higher-ups in the RCMP should have realized this situation could have been resolved over a year previously, before the division between one female and several male officers had become polarized. To this day I do not understand why people and organizations can't accept mistakes and move on.

Early resolution took a few short months once the Canadian Human Rights Complaint was sent, I was more than willing to get to my new detachment. My resignation stopped in Ottawa and I was looking forward to my new detachment. My complaints within the RCMP had fallen on deaf ears. To survive in the RCMP I had to go to an outside agency, something the organization was not accustomed. I am easy to get along with, but mess with me and I will be your worst nightmare. The RCMP will only come to realize this as I submit another complaint to the Canadian Human Rights Commission in Ottawa, and forward a Statement of Claim to the Federal Court in 2006. The bureaucracy in the RCMP stays the same and my transfer to Selkirk Highway Patrol in 1992 was the beginning of another journey on the road to survival in the RCMP.

Introduction To Death

I ARRIVED AT SELKIRK HIGHWAY PATROL IN DECEMBER 1992, and I simply wanted to go to work every day, go home to my daughter and remain anonymous. After the grueling experience of Tisdale, I wanted and needed peace of mind. This was not meant to be.

When I arrived at Selkirk Detachment, I felt welcomed by most of the officers. A few viewed me as a troublemaker because of the manner in which I had been transferred from Tisdale, and parachuted into Selkirk. Sergeant Dave Edmundson was a kind-hearted man with over 25 years of service, and now ready to retire. Corporal Wallen had a big moustache, a kind and gentle nature and was also ready to retire. I liked their sense of humour and humanity. Both these officers helped guide me to be an effective officer while I was on Highway Patrol. When they retired within a year the whole atmosphere of the detachment began to change, and not for the better.

A few of the officers did not respect their female partners and referred to me as "Barbie" for my blond hair and "Copper Top" for a short period when I dyed it red. This name-calling was further evidence of the lack of respect some officers had for female officers. I ignored these comments for a while as the Tisdale experience was still fresh in my memory. However, when the comments continued with laughter from one of the other officers, it was evident my credibility as an equal was being eroded. When asked to stop the name calling one officer refused. Finally, during one afternoon I had enough. I turned to this officer and retorted, "Is that your face, or did your neck throw up?"

Needless to say, the other officers howled with laughter. It was his turn to be embarrassed. Being polite did not work, and ignoring the comments did not work, I had to stand up to him, and finally stop the name calling by tossing him an insult. The name-calling stopped.

There are events in a police officer's life that are never forgotten and mine was my first investigation of a fatal car accident. One cloudy spring Sunday afternoon in May, while on a highway about 25 kilometers north of Winnipeg, the members of Selkirk Highway patrol were conducting a traffic stop, checking for seatbelt violations, licenses and open liquor. A car pulled up to us and the driver looked visibly upset. He said he had just passed a terrible car accident, south of the check stop and he thought someone could be hurt. We immediately got into our police cars and sped back to the scene.

It was a sight I will never forget! Two cars were involved, the larger car in the centre median, on its side, in the grass. The other smaller vehicle had been coming east, failed to stop at the intersection and was struck on the driver's side. The force had propelled the vehicle into the north bound lane. I raced to the smaller vehicle where I could see four occupants. An elderly female driver appeared to be dead, her head leaning back on the head rest; her eyes glazed over and still, skin grey and white. The driver's side window had broken glass indicating that she had smashed against the driver's door, the impact killing her instantly. I moved in close to her face as I touched her neck in desperate hope of finding a pulse, but her life was over. Her husband was crying and holding her hand. I let him stay with his wife. The crying sounds blended with sounds of the police sirens, ambulances in the distance, and the voices of many officers at the scene.

There were two elderly women in the back seat of the car, one of whom appeared to be dead. I could tell that the force of the impact had caused this woman to be thrown upwards forcing the hatchback door to break off the hinges. Such force could have caused multiple neck and head injuries. When I spoke to the other elderly woman in the back seat to determine any injuries, I noticed her face was grey in color, she said she felt sick. She kept repeating words that made no sense and I could tell she was in shock. I looked for obvious injuries but could not see any blood or protruding bones. My stomach felt sick, with tightness heretofore unknown to me. I kept thinking of what to do next, there were so many injured and two dead. The sound for which I prayed was the distant ambulance finally getting closer. I tried to get the man to let go of his wife and reassured him, "You will be okay, the ambulance is on the way." I was ashamed I could not see what was happening for him. His words brought tears to my eyes: "How can I be okay? I have lost my best friend and love!" I heard him, the words and the pain, so I let go of his arm and moved toward the injured woman in the back seat. More police cars arrived to assist with the injured and with traffic control. The woman in the backseat was trying to climb out of the car and another officer made her sit down on the grass to wait for the ambulance. I explained the ambulance was coming and to stay still. An ambulance arrived after what seemed an eternity and the two occupants of the much larger car, a father and son, who had sustained only minor injuries, and taken away.

Another ambulance was to come and collect the two fatalities. It was a busy Sunday afternoon and as vehicles drove by the accident, many curious drivers slowed down to see the tragedy. Out of respect for the victims, I covered the bodies with yellow body blankets to prevent the public from staring with morbid fascination. Yellow blankets are used, as they are reflective and can be seen in the dark. I needed help and asked my partner, John, to assist with this gruesome task.

As I covered the driver and moved her head slightly to tuck the blanket under her head, the back of her head fell away and the contents of her brain began to slip out. The sound it made was the same as one hears when stepping out of wet mud with a rubber boot, that slopping, slurping sound. There was a disgusting odour I can't explain in words. It was so strong both my partner and I began to gag. I was so angry at myself for this weakness. What would the public think of me as a police officer if I threw up on a body? I looked up, took a big breath and finished wrapping her head in the body blanket, then stumbled backward and gagged. I felt terrible about my reaction. I had no idea this is quite a normal reaction to such a scene. All the training in the world can not prepare a person for such an experience.

Another ambulance arrived and removed the two fatalities. I went to the hospital shortly after covering the bodies. Family members told me the three women in the smaller car were related, the driver having been married to the male passenger. The survivors from both cars eventually recovered from their injuries. I felt the tremendous sense of loss one would feel losing two sisters in one disaster. I have three sisters myself and could not imagine the pain of losing two of them in a single day.

The scene was cleaned up, cars were removed, but the memories haunt me to this day. Every time I drive by this intersection, I see the little car with a man crying over his dead wife and I imagine the loss he must be living daily. In remembering this incident, I want to make sure I don't become so bitter with life that I can no longer feel the sting of pain it evokes. The family members were thankful I was kind to their father. One of my supervisors gave me the name Constable 'Heart' because of the gentle manner in which I treated the public.

On a few occasions, I was asked to return items to family members of victims who had died in car accidents. One occasion in partic-ular remains vivid in my memory. A father came to collect his daugh-ter's purse; she had been a passenger with two male companions and the driver was impaired. All three had been killed the previous night in a head-on collision with another car. The two occupants of the other car also died. I came to work the following morning and was told to return this purse to a man. I did not know of the accident but soon checked the daily log. I read about the accident and the multiple victims. The father was coming in to retrieve the girl's belongings. A highway patrol officer told me to return the purse as "You're better at it." What he really wanted to say, but could not was, 'I can't handle it but I know you can.'

I collected the purse and wiped off some of the blood and pre-pared myself for any possible reaction from the father. When he came to the detachment I had no idea what to say to him. I am a mother with one daughter and could not imagine the pain he was feeling at this moment. He walked into the detachment through front door and stood behind the bullet proof glass which separated the public from the inner office.

I opened the door leading out to where he was standing; I wanted to speak with him face to face, not through the impersonal and sterile glass. His eyes were all red and puffy. I said the first thing that came to mind, "I am so sorry for your loss."

He looked at me for a few seconds, lost his composure and he started to cry, his head dropping down. I reached out and held him. This grown man cried like a small child, clinging to me as if I was somehow able to bring back his daughter. At that moment, I wished I could turn back time and change what had happened. I let him cry and said nothing. A nauseated feeling began building in my stomach: it was such a waste of human life. After several minutes, the father slowly pulled back and without looking at me said, "Thanks."

I just nodded and quietly gave him the purse and asked if he was going to be okay. My concern was his ability to drive, as he was so distraught. He explained that a relative had driven him to the detachment. I offered my assistance if he needed someone to talk to. He shook my hand and left with the last thing his daughter had held, her purse. I watched him get into the car, then walked back into the detachment and said I was going for coffee. One of the other officers said, "You sure took a long time with that guy." I drove out of town, parked on the shoulder of the road and cried. I cried for me, I cried for father and the young woman who will never have her life. To this day I hate the excuses drunk drivers give in court after they have killed someone.

Another time I returned a child's belongings resulting from a fatality involving a bike and car. A small child was biking down his driveway onto the road and did not see an oncoming car, was struck and wedged under the car. He was smothered to death as his face was pressed against the road. Several days later, the file on this incident was concluded with no charges against the driver. The child's belongings were to be returned to the grieving parents. They had one child and now he was gone forever. As the parents waited in the lobby of the detachment I got the child's belongings. The child's baseball cap was in an exhibit bag and I noticed there was blood splatter on it, so before giving it to the parents, I gently asked if they would like me to clean the hat first. They were appreciative of my consideration so I went to the washroom and cleaned off the blood, wiping the cap, trying to remove the red stain. The cap represented a son who was loved and cherished. It broke my heart to see the parents in such heart-wrenching pain as the mother clutched the hat in her hands. In my opinion, methods of dealing with these situations are not taught in sufficient detail at the academy in Regina, and as you can see there certainly is a need.

Back on Patrol

I HAD AN INTERESTING EXPERIENCE ON EVENING PATROL in the fall of 1993. I was alone on highway patrol and told to go as far as Gimli, work a couple of hours then head back to the Selkirk detachment. I worked on Highway 9 in the Gimli area and because I was close to home had supper with my daughter before heading back to Selkirk to end my night shift. As I was driving south on Highway 9 I noticed a red car approaching and swerving all over the road. I pulled over on the shoulder to make sure I did not get hit, turned my police car around in pursuit, and activated the police lights. However, the driver continued on and only stopped when I put on the roof lights and siren. I approached the vehicle, a red BMW, with a lone female driver about 65 years of age at the wheel. I asked where she was going. She turned to look at me and I could instantly smell what was similar to nail polish. Her eyes were trying to focus on my face and when she spoke, her heavy French accent made her difficult to understand. I was not sure whether she was intoxicated or not? Perhaps something else was causing her to swerve on the road. I needed to ask more questions to determine whether she was, in fact, an impaired driver. She kept rolling her head from side to side as she spoke.

Her response confirmed my suspicion, "I am heading back home, to Winnipeg. I just came from the dentist and, as you can see, the braces are painful. This is highway 8, no?" Not only was she going in the wrong direction, on the wrong highway, but she was in Gimli, a population of 1500, not Winnipeg. As well, highway #8 is a double lane. I asked for her driver's license. As she fumbled in her purse I noticed she had a 10 once vodka bottle which appeared to be half full. Suddenly I recognized the smell from her breath, it was vodka. She must have been drinking it straight from the bottle.

I arrested her for impaired driving and placed her in the back of my police car. She stumbled getting into the back seat. The woman was tall, beautifully dressed in an expensive suit, groomed to the nines, owned an expensive car and was drinking straight vodka in her car. I wondered what was happening in her life to make her do something so dangerous.

I took her to the Gimli detachment for the breathalyzer. I had to have another officer do the test as I had not taken the course. The longer I was with her, the more intoxicated she appeared. She was swearing at me in French, rolling her head from side to side. She repeated several times, "You can't do this to me, I am a doctor, I am on pain killers for my teeth. Can't you see this!" Upon making further inquires, I confirmed she was a doctor and in her purse was a prescription for pain. She must have mixed the drug with the vodka. In order to be released after the test, she needed to have a sober adult come to get her. She asked for her husband who had to drive from Winnipeg with another driver, to pick her up. Usually, the court documents are served on the individual prior to release but she was intoxicated I decided to serve her the next day in Winnipeg. I did not wait in Gimli for her husband to pick her up. She remained in custody waiting for him, and I returned to Selkirk at the end of my shift. I have often wondered about the people I had arrested for impaired driving and whether being arrested had made them choose not to drink and drive. I hope so.

Life on Selkirk Highway patrol was fun. I enjoyed the work and my fellow officers. One officer who liked traffic enforcement as much as I did was Corporal Hawkeye. His nickname was 'Hawk Cop' because he was so good at his job on traffic enforcement. He liked to do roadblocks and stopped hundreds of cars while looking for various violations, such as not wearing a seat belt, children not in seat belts, lack of valid licenses and registration. Sometimes we would get a suspended driver, open liquor or drugs. The roadblocks done at night in the freezing winter were a killer. The RCMP issue boots did not keep my feet warm. I knew that on our night shifts, Corporal Hawkeye wanted to do roadblocks for several hours at a time. Most often I was so cold, I could not feel my feet. I had bought hand warmers for my car emergency pack for my daughter and myself when we went on road trips. I decided to get some for my feet and use them at work.

Next nightshift I arrived at the detachment and just before Corporal Hawkeye and I left to set up the roadblock, I put the hot packs in my boots, under my feet, and one in each mitt. My body was toasty warm for the five hours we were outside in the -35 winter night. Other officers asked why I looked so happy while they were miserable, freezing with chattering teeth. I just smiled.

My First Shooting

I HAD TO DRAW MY GUN SEVERAL OCCASIONS DURING my service. Prior to my injury, one evening shift while returning from the northern town of Grand Marais, I was alone in one police car, and my supervisor and another officer were patrolling together in another. We had stopped to have coffee with some officers from the Grand Marais detachment and it was dark by the time we headed back to Selkirk. I was following my supervisor and as his car pulled farther ahead, he called on the radio to tell me about a big white bag in the middle of the road. He suggested I stop and move it so other cars coming around the corner wouldn't swerve or get into car accidents. I came around the corner and saw the white bag. I activated my emergency lights to ensure oncoming cars were aware of my presence. As I and walked up to the bag, I realized it was a huge, white, longhaired dog lying on the yellow line. It looked dead. I radioed back to my supervisor that it was a dog. He said, "Pull it off into the ditch." I walked up to the dog and as I grabbed the two back legs, pulled hard. The dog lifted his head and howled a death howl. I could see by the eyes it was in pain. One eye was closed and the other was partially open but dropping down and blood was coming from the mouth and ear. I nearly had a heart attack and dropped the legs. I called my supervisor and told him about the dog's condition. He said "CX it." I asked, "What does that mean?" A voice came from another officer who had been listening and patrolling out in the area, "Double tap." 'Double tap' is a term used in RCMP firearms training. The 'double tap' is shooting two shots quickly to bring down a suspect permanently. Was he was saying I was to kill it? I had to shoot this poor animal? I walked up to the animal wishing I had been in the first car and still driving home. I looked up and noticed a man walking towards me from a nearby driveway. He said he had heard the screeching of brakes and was worried about his dog. My heart sank. He had not seen the white mass lying on the yellow line on the road. I asked what type of dog it was, hoping there was another dog but he described the white dog. I moved to stand between him and the dying dog. Reluctantly I told him his dog had been hit, was barely alive and seriously injured. The man looked visibly upset. I asked if he wanted me to end the suffering of the poor animal. He offered to do it but would need to get his shot gun. The flashing blue and red lights of the police car showed the pain on the man's face. His eyes filled with tears. "Oh my God, here comes my wife, she loves the dog!" I could see another person walking towards us so I suggested he tell her before she came too close, as it would only upset her more to see her pet suffering. I watched as he walked up the driveway to meet his wife. I could hear her start to cry. Holding each other, they walked up to the house and both went inside. Several minutes later the man came out with his shot gun. As he approached I could see the strain on his face. We stood over the dog as it howled in pain. He looked at me, "I'm sorry, I can't do it. Can you do it?" There was hesitation in his voice. I felt so sad for him. I remembered the feeling of loss when my own dog had died. He looked at me, then at the dog, then at his gun. I knew immediately, he wanted to give me the shot gun. I felt dread. I had been told in training and at the detachment that occasionally police officers have to end the suffering of animals.

"No thanks, I can use my own. Perhaps you want to wait behind my car." I motioned to the back of my police cruiser. He nodded and walked behind the police car. I ensured there was no traffic coming, removed my gun from the holster and pointed at the back of the white head. I felt I could not do it either, I had no courage. Just because I am a police officer doesn't mean I like doing this but I had no choice. The dog lifted its head, looked at me and howled. Along desperate sound echoed in the darkness. It was his way of giving me the strength. I knew I could not stand to hear that sound again. I gently pulled the trigger. The dog started to howl as the sound of the second bullet echoed all around us. Then the dog lay still. The sick smell of blood mixed with gun power was nauseating. I gagged as I holstered my weapon then walked behind the car. I suggested we put the dog on a body bag, (yellow plastic) to drag it off the road. The man had his hands over his ears. Once he saw me, knew it was over. I repeated my suggestion. In addition, I felt if the body were covered, his wife would not have to see all the blood pooling on the road. I got the body bag and together we pulled the dog into the bag and dragged it off the road. The deep red trail behind the dog's body was reflected in the flash of the coloured police lights.

The man thanked me for helping his dog. He hugged me and with drooping shoulders walked back to his house. The front door was open and the woman came running out for comfort. They held onto each other. He said they would bury the dog in the morning. I did not feel like I had helped anyone. As I watched them walk up the front steps and into the house, the smell of gun powder and blood filled my nostrils and I felt sick to my stomach. After taking several deep breaths, got into the car and drove away.

This incident changed me. I never thought I could kill. The sensation of pulling the trigger and knowing the bullet is going into a body is sickening. I hoped I would never have this experience again. The thought of shooting a dog was bad enough let alone a human.

Who Would Help Me?

UPON MY ARRIVAL IN SELKIRK IN DECEMBER 1992, AND beginning in January 1993, I stayed under the radar of the other officers and tried to be inconspicuous while still fitting in. However, I was young and attractive and some of the men had different ideas. They teased, joked and flirted, and I enjoyed this attention, thinking and hoping this made me belong. After surviving Tisdale, I tried to remain anonymous. During my service with the RCMP I learned that some male officers have a variety of classifications for the female officers. Single women are categorized as sex machines, ugly, lesbian or frigid.

One officer, Larry G., whom I had met upon my arrival, was unrelenting in his pursuit to get me into bed. I distrusted him imme-diately as he appeared to have a new girlfriend every week and I did not want that type of relationship. Larry G. was not bad looking, about 5' 10," moustache, thinning dark hair and a pear-shaped body. He was not the physical fitness type that I like. He had a video which was the topic of many conversations. This video showed Larry G. engaging in sex with two women who, he claimed, were a mother and daughter. This video was common knowledge and he boasted openly about his girlfriends and complained when the relationship did not work out. I did not hide my displeasure. I am not attracted to loud people and I questioned the mental state of anyone who wants to watch this type of display. I had not been exposed to such narcissistic sexual sociopath from a guy before. When he asked if I wanted to watch the video with him, I politely said "No thank you".

Some of the other officers thought Larry G. and I would make a great couple. I thought this bizarre as I did not appreciate his attitude toward women. After a few months at the detachment, he began making an effort to join Highway Patrol for coffee, sit beside me, and assist me in road checks. We had several conversations about work, family and relationships. I was under the impression that he wanted to change his attitude towards women and dating. He frequently would ask for my opinion on what I thought was romantic and what type of man I was looking for. Trusting him was a huge mistake.

Larry G. had backed me up on a few calls and I began to trust him as a fellow officer and friend. This was my first mistake. My second mistake was having drinks with him and some other officers at the end of an evening shift. I had a couple of drinks with fellow officers to unwind from the hectic week and the stress of my first double fatal, remembering the four victims in the one car, the husband crying over his dead wife, wiping the blood from her face and hand, and saying she was beautiful. I spent the week washing the smell of death from my body. I dreamed of the dead eyes staring back as I had checked for a pulse. It had been a terribly trying week emotionally.

I was also feeling lonely and tired. Being a single mother is tough and because I am a police officer, some of my dates leave skid marks racing out the door trying to get away when they heard how I made my living.

After a few drinks I decided it was not safe for me to drive home. Larry G. said I could crash at his house for a few hours and he would drive me back to my car. He had a spare bedroom and I needed some time for the drinks to wore off. I probably could have driven home as I was the last highway patrol officer on duty and Larry G. was the last rural officer. But I don't like the idea of drinking and driving. I have a little girl who looks up to me. The last thing that I wanted was to be in a car accident and lying on the road all night until the light of day when some stranger driving by sees my mangled body.

Larry G. also promised to be a complete gentleman. Ted came for a drink as well that evening. I was more attracted to Ted because he was cute and funny but he was also married. I was really tired and wanted to sleep. Larry G. showed me to the bedroom and gave me a pair of long gym shorts to wear instead of my uniform. I was so tired I flopped into bed. Soon I heard the door open and Larry G. and Ted came in to the room. I just kind of moaned and sighed in my tired and alcohol state as they stood at the foot of the bed. Larry G. was talking to Ted. I felt uncomfortable with them standing there but was too tired to do or say anything. Larry G. did have some charming qualities, but mostly he was a bragging, sex hungry loud mouth with a big butt. Not my type. I could hear them leave the room and I briefly I fell asleep. I know Larry G. came back into the room because I awoke with him beside me. He lay down beside me on top of the covers. He was talking about how beautiful I was, and that "going without sex for a woman is not normal." My physical response was one of revulsion. I felt completely trapped. My intoxicated brain scrambled to find words, my body unable to get up and run as he pulled down the safety of the blanket, exposing me. I remember thinking he has an ugly body, pear shaped and un attractive. I don't want to do this. The only words that escaped from my mouth were in a powerless quiet pleading whisper, "Don't, please I just want to sleep, don't I ,I I, could get pregnant". In my mind, I was screaming for him to stop, and go away, but there was no voice. I just thought what happens if I get pregnant because of this assault? I would die. Larry G. took advantage of the situation, he sexually assaulted me. I felt awful and quickly dressed, leaving like the house was on fire. I asked to be driven back to the detachment to get my car. I had to get out of the room, the house and away from this disgusting man. Sitting in the police car as he drove me back to the detachment, I felt like such a loser, how could I let this happen to me? At that time I believed it was my fault. I had the drinks, I came to his house, I didn't fight or scream and he was police officer. Once at the detachment I got to the safety of my car and I left him sitting in the police car. Without saying a word I drove home feeling more violated than I ever felt before. I sped out the detachment parking lot like a bat out of hell, just wanting to get home and shower. To this day I never go to parties where there are no other female officers, and the only man that I drink alone with is my husband, David.

It was like a bad dream. Once at home, I showered and went to bed feeling drained, my skin red, raw in the attempt to scrub away the attack. It was as if I wanted to mold my legs together and never allow anyone touch me. Upon waking my first memory was of the attack. A flood of nausea came over me. I had to put on a brave face as I played with Nadine and had coffee with my family. My mind was filled with fear and impending doom, I had to go to work tonight, and he would be there. I wanted to kill him for what he did. I was afraid for myself, afraid of my growing hate and sense of betrayal. It would be easy to walk up behind him and pull the trigger into his ugly head. No other woman would fall victim and become his sexual prey. At the time I did not realize this hate is an emotion that all rape victims feel, especially when they had trusted the attacker.

I had to remember Nadine needed me to care for her. At that moment I began to bury the memory of the night before, deep, so deep in the blackness of my mind. It was several years later and with counseling I was able to accept what had happened and heal. As evening approached, while driving to Selkirk, I had a panic attack in the car. My heart was beating so hard it hurt, my hands were sweaty and my tongue and feet weighed a ton. In the parking lot I had to take a couple of deep breaths to calm down. I wondered, "what was wrong with me?" I unlocked the back door and could hear his voice from the coffee room upstairs. I could hear him bragging about his sexual conquest the night before, and not of the rape that had really occurred. I wanted to run to my car and go away, but my feet were stuck in the doorway. Stuck and unable to move or speak when suddenly the sound of boots on the stairs made me jump back to reality and I walked to my desk. As the officers from Rural detachment came down the stairs and brushed past me the panic in my stomach was all consuming. The attacker Larry G. and the other officers were coming down the stairs from the coffee room. They were laughing, "Well, it couldn't have happened to a nicer guy." Then they noticed me and, with an uncomfortable "Hi," they walked by. I wanted to disappear, out of shame. I felt sick to my stomach and humiliated that I could have been abused by a fellow police officer. Someone I trusted. I took the police car and stayed away from the detachment for most of the shift. I am sure this was not the first time he had done this and probably not the last time a woman had fallen victim to him. "No consent" means it is an assault. I had wanted justice but denial, fear and humiliation kept me quiet.

Many years later, he got what he deserved. He was charged, convicted with a crime and fired from the RCMP. He suffered complete and utter public humiliation. I have often thought of going after him legally, possibly seeking out other victims. It would be sweet revenge on a character disorder hiding in a RCMP uniform.

Ted had asked me a few weeks later about Larry G. because he had heard 'the rumours.' I felt my face go red but looked him straight in the eye and said, "Well, I guess it must be a great conquest, forcing yourself on someone who is not willing or interested and had been drinking." My chest was tight with the memory of fear and the shame. It was his turn to go red in the face. He knew exactly what I meant, that Larry G. had sexually assaulted me and there was no consent. Who would believe me? I had been drinking; I went to his house and even to the bedroom. If this went to court, the defense would demolish me. I felt I could not come forward and press charges. I had just survived Tisdale. How would I survive coming forward with a complaint of sexual assault against a fellow RCMP officer? Who would help me? The RCMP?

My self-esteem took a tailspin from this assault, and as a result, I experienced a couple of less than satisfying relationships with attached men. Memories of the assault demoralized me and made me feel like damaged goods. I believed I was undeserving of having a loving, faithful relationship and this affected my choice of boyfriends. I was looking for intimacy and thought sex would fulfill this need. How wrong I was. I ended up feeling even more alone and empty than before. The experiences I had lived through had affected my sense of identity. I repressed feelings of romantic inadequacy during this period of time and managed to find a measure of fulfillment in my job as a police officer, and my role as a mother.

Shotgun Blast
That Changed My Future

MY LIFE AND MY CAREER PATH CHANGED IN SEPTEMBER of 1994, at the Annual RCMP firearms qualifications. As police officers, we are required to carry firearms and qualify annually. An officer who does not qualify should not be in a police car. All officers need to be proficient in firing the weapon that may save a life. There were several other officers qualifying with the handgun and shotgun.

My experience with the shotgun was fraught with anxiety. The reason for this was simple: in Regina, during training, the firearms instructor thought a few of us girls (four) needed to get over our fear of the shotgun so he ordered us to remain after class to "learn to love the shotgun." He made us shoot twenty-five shotgun slugs in a row. A shogun slug has a powerful kick. I thought I was going to die. The recoil to my right shoulder felt like getting hit with a hammer. My body shook with the impact, the butt of the gun rammed into my body, giving me a huge bruise lasting weeks. With each shot, I closed my eyes and just pulled the trigger. The sooner I finished my rounds of slugs, the sooner I could leave and get ice to my arm and shoulder.

At the end of this session, I was shooting with my eyes squeezed shut in anticipation of pain in my shoulder. At supper in the mess that night, none of us could even lift a fork. It took a weekend of ice and heat to mend our bodies.

I had practiced several times for the annual firearms qualifications with the shotgun since graduation in 1989. However, my fear had by now somewhat subsided. To protect myself from the recoil and impact I would wear my bulletproof vest and pack some socks under my vest to cover the area where the stock of the gun pressed up against my shoulder. In Tisdale at the annual shoot, we had shooting jackets, which resembled a coat, with thick leather on each side covering the shoulder area. I used this jacket in Tisdale and did not have any trouble qualifying. However, this jacket was not available at the shoot in Selkirk. To this day, I don't know what mistake I made in holding the shotgun or even if I made a mistake.

The Annual Firearms qualifications included two firearms instructors and about sixteen officers. We each used our service weapons, were given a target and needed to be accurate to get a certain mark in order to qualify. The target is the silhouette of a man and the objective is to shoot closet to the heart. Each part of the silhouette is marked by numbers. The closer the shot to the heart or center mass, the higher the number or point. To qualify each officer has to maintain a certain number of points. There are several different positions from which to shoot in order to simulate real life. There are standing, kneeling positions, using the right hand beside a barricade, and then using the left hand. The scores are important. If an officer fails to qualify, he or she is required to return and complete the entire process again another day. Failing could result in termination of duties. I don't want a partner who can't shoot and back me up.

At the shoot we take turns, about eight at a time, standing in a row with our own individual targets down the firing line, all wearing ear protectors. Qualifying with the shotgun was different this time for me.

We were required to drive up in a police car, jump out and shoot at the target. This was fun but the few shells we used were not slugs. The difference between a shotgun shell and a slug is the amount of lead. A slug is one big pellet and the recoil is like a horse kick. A normal shotgun shell has a kick but is not unbearable. Once all the officers had completed the driving and shooting exercise, we moved to shooting shotgun slugs in the standing position.

I fired a couple of times and with the third shot, suddenly felt my upper body split in two. The gun flew back and up into my face, hitting my mouth. I tasted blood but that was nothing compared to the searing pain in my right shoulder. My arm hung limp at my side. At first, I thought my collar bone was broken. My right arm just hung there. I cradled it in my left arm. I knew I had to finish the rounds still in the gun or come back and complete the qualification another day, which I did not feel I could endure. I managed to get the gun to my shoulder and finish the rounds. At that point hitting the target was not a worry. I dropped the gun and let my arm fall. The pain was excruciating. One of the firearms supervisors came up to me and commented that I looked sick and pale.

I felt nauseated. The firearms instructors suggested I go to the hospital. I was driven to the Selkirk Hospital by another officer, examined by a doctor and released. Initially it was thought I had broken my collar bone, but thankfully it was not broken. I was given some Tylenol 3s for pain.

The prognosis was possibly a bruised shoulder, deep tissue bruising, and a slight dislocation. An officer from highway patrol drove me in my car back to my home as I could not drive. In fact, the injury was more serious than at first thought, because I had pulled and stretched the muscles that hold my arm in place. The rotator cuff had been damaged, and could not support the bone, so my arm would roll out of place many times a day or night whenever I was relaxed. This resulted in excruciating pain that made me scream, and then my muscles would tighten causing the arm to roll back into place. To this day I have not had a good night's sleep due to discomfort and tossing and turning from the shoulder pain.

After the initial injury, I was off work for a few days and returned to office duties while waiting to see an orthopedic surgeon, Dr. De-Comby. I received two sets of steroid injections in the shoulder. However, the pain, lack of movement and strength did not improve. Several weeks later I went for an exploratory surgery, where my shoulder was frozen, a thin needle inserted and a dye injected to determine the type of injury I had. This was when it was discovered I had torn muscles, rotator cuff damage and a destabilized shoulder. Dr. DeComby put me on light duties, which is administrative or paperwork, as I was not able to do operational police work, which is being out in the police car. I was assigned administration duties from October 1994 to the day before my surgery in March 1995.

My surgery was successful. This followed by ten months of physiotherapy. The injury had destabilized my shoulder and the surgery had secured the muscles and bone. However, after the months of physiotherapy, I had not gained much in the way of mobility with the right shoulder. At this point I could not move my arm over my head. A second surgery under general anesthetic was required to force the muscles to move and to increase mobility. This second surgery done on January 10, 1996, was again followed by eight months of physiotherapy, recovery and pain. I returned to Selkirk and to office work in May of 1996.

Later the same year it was determined the injury was permanent and I could no longer be considered for full operational duties, front line policing and working in the police car. I had no idea the next few years were going to be a real challenge. Problems with my right shoulder continue to cause pain and limit mobility to this day.

Where Is The Equality?

AFTER MUCH INVESTIGATION OF THE RCMP'S POLICIES and practices of past history, I was surprised by the fact the RCMP had made many 'accommodations' for male officers but appeared less than receptive to giving me the same consideration with regard to my duty related shoulder injury. I expected to be treated equally and fairly and would not allow the RCMP to bully me or force me to quit. The inconsistencies of decisions by management and "accommodation" choices between injured male and female officers was an issue I would continue to address. This I believe, surprised the RCMP that I was actively doing something about this discrimination. My tenacity would not let me stop in my quest. I had no idea that my grievance would last six years and beyond or that there would be significant changes in the policies within our organization.

I forwarded a Level 1 Grievance in September 1997, against the Medical Discharge proceedings. My argument was the RCMP had made "accommodations" for male officers who had sustained injuries in both duty and non-duty related accidents; therefore I should also be 'accommodated', treated equally. Once again, the RCMP did not respond. A few weeks after my grievance was forwarded and the paper work sent in, I was required to provide other documents relating to my file at the Gimli Detachment. These documents were to be handed to the Officer in Command, Superintendent Kline, of Gimli Sub Division, who I recall asking me why I had forwarded the grievance in the first place. He was a tall man with an intimidating presence. My response was. "I want what is best for me." He replied, "Have you thought of what is best for the RCMP?"

I just stared in disbelief as he spoke. Apparently, officers in the RCMP believed I was actually hurting the organization by not agreeing to the Medical Discharge. In their mind, my grievance being viewed as a personal attack against the RCMP organization. Superintendent Kline's response only reaffirmed my initial conclusion on the intelligence of some RCMP officers, which was once they reach the higher ranks, don't really care about the wellbeing of the front line officers. He was a Superintendent, making over $100,000 per year or more and could look forward to a hefty pension. I, on the other hand, had less than ten years service as a constable with no money and no pension and I had a small child. He had the audacity to expect me to think of the Force and what my grievance may do to it.

Looking back, I think whenever I was confronted with stupidity in the Force, it only served to reinforce my determination to go forward. I continued to follow the path that in my mind was a quest for fair and equal treatment. If my ancestors who emigrated from Iceland to Canada only to face, small pox, famine and discrimination, had given up, there would be no Icelanders in Canada and no me.

I had worked hard to become an RCMP officer and was not about to get tossed about. I actually enjoyed being on highway patrol where I got to be my own boss, promoting good police relations with the general public. My shifts consisted of patrolling our detachment area, enforcing traffic laws, setting up and manning road blocks, checking for seatbelts, driver's licenses, open liquor, suspended and impaired drivers. It was gratifying when I nailed an impaired driver, knowing I was potentially saving lives, either of the drunk driver or anyone else who might have gotten injured or killed.

The Selkirk Highway Patrol and Selkirk Rural detachments were in the same building, with Patrol on one side of the building and Rural on the other. We shared equipment and the assistance of support staff. Staff would come and go during the time I was stationed on patrol. The retirement of Sergeant Dave Edmundson and Corporal Wallen allowed for new supervisors who were not as kind or understanding. One such boss was Sergeant Bruce MacKinnon, a twin to Chilton in that he appeared to be a vain dictator who loved to gossip. He did not like anyone asking questions about his decisions. I found him to be unprofessional and a bully, who was allowed to get away with this behaviour because no one ever challenged him.

SHERRY LEE BENSON-PODOLCHUK

106

Not All Lawyers Are Useless

I STARTED TO TAKE CHARGE OF MY FUTURE BY HIRING A lawyer in 1996, Mr. Roger Bond, from Winnipeg. He was referred to me by another RCMP officer with whom I had gone to university in 1988. After my injury and second surgery, I decided to get legal advice and prepare the groundwork for any possible complications with the RCMP. I sent copies of all documents to Roger who gave me advice as to changes needed, and I myself prepared the letter. This way I saved a great deal of money, Roger stayed in the background in the legal battle until I was served Notice of Medical Discharge in 1997. I had been off work with my injury and the two surgeries from March 1995 to May 1996. My right shoulder had a permanent injury from the RCMP annual Firearms qualification back in September of 1994.

During that time, between the initial 1994 injury, and the subsequent surgeries and then my return to work in May 1996, there was a flurry of paper work going back and forth between the RCMP Staffing office at D Division (this including various Inspectors at D Division, other RCMP officers), my lawyer and me. The Staffing officer wanted

SHERRY LEE BENSON-PODOLCHUK

to determine if, in the future, my shoulder would improve and allow me to return to full operational duties, that being a front line police officer. The surgeon, Dr. DeComby, sent a letter advising the RCMP of the extent of the permanent damage to my shoulder, which made it impossible for me to return to operational duties. He indicated that there was limited mobility in my shoulder and external rotation of 80%. The shoulder muscles were also weakened.

I had sent memos to D Division during this time and for years after to the staffing office and administration offices, with suggestions as to alternative duties I would be able to perform, such as Customs and Excise, Immigration and Passport, Media Relations, and Victim Services. They refused to consider any of these, nor did they offer any further ideas. Dr. Pivot of the RCMP Health Services told me, "Basically, my dear, you are useless."

RCMP policy is that when an officer is injured and cannot return to full duties, they do a division search, then a Canada-wide search for a position and, if nothing is found, they issue a Medical Discharge. Nothing was found. I forwarded a grievance on the grounds the RCMP did not provide an adequate division and nation wide job search. It was a one lined sentence, faxed to each Division Staffing office across Canada with no mention of the type of injury or any indication of my skills and abilities. This effort by the RCMP in conducting a search was pathetic, poorly done and eventually would become part of my second grievance. In order for a Division Staffing office to determine a suitable position for an officer, they require detail as to the type of injury, recovery, knowledge and skills in other policing areas. None of this completed.

During the time of the job search, I remained on light duties at Selkirk Highway Patrol, which essentially consisted of secretarial jobs. Officers would dump administrative work on my desk and expect me to be grateful for it. This was frustrating because I became reduced to an assistant to the secretarial staff and no longer viewed as a police officer. The Sergeant in charge of Highway Patrol did not like the fact that he had an officer who could not go out and generate tickets. He began to pick at my efforts by leaving sarcastic comments on my work. Remembering Tisdale, four years earlier, I could see where this was going. I did not want to go through that hell again and tried to remain calm in spite of the Sergeant's very public incessant finickiness and sarcastic tone. For example, a complaint might come in of a car swerving on the road and if the complainant is not willing to go to court to testify as to what occurred, then there is no case. The Sergeant would get angry with me if the witness did not want to give a statement. I would try to explain that some witnesses will never come to the office for statements and the thought of going to court is terrifying. The Sergeant did not like me defending myself when he made remarks on my file and I would send the file back with my comments. I did this because it was important to have written proof of what I could see as a repeat of Tisdale treatment and performance report.

After several months of this harassing behaviour, I sent a letter dated January 1997, to Inspector W. Holland of the RCMP Sub Division in Gimli advising him of my work situation. We met to arrange a transfer for me to the Gimli detachment. I thought perhaps another beginning and felt happy about this new opportunity. I was very much aware of what can happen in a work environment where the workers and supervisor are not supportive. Also, my daughter was going to school in Gimli and I could drop her off at school on my way to work and I could pick her up at the end of the day.

I enjoyed my time in Gimli Detachment and hoped a position would be found for me so I would not lose my financial independence. During coffee one morning, I was informed of Staff/Sergeant Cullen recent heart attack and although he was unfit for operational duties, he was fit for administration and would maintain his job. This surprised and angered me and I questioned the Inspector why the RCMP was being selective regarding who is 'accommodated' and who is not. He offered no response. In February 1997, when Sergeant Bruce MacKinnon visited Gimli Detachment, he called me aside and told me that a Notice of Medical Discharge paper had been sent to him to serve on me. Within a day, he telephoned to advise that D Division Staffing had called him requesting the papers be returned, as there had been a mistake in sending the document to me in the first place. This came as a complete shock to me. I called Sergeant Doby from Administration and Personnel office at D Division, to inquire about the papers. He advised me they were sent in error and I was not to have seen them. I told him I had a copy and I had promptly sent it to my lawyer, Roger.

It seemed like the sky fell on me when served the Notice to Medical Discharge in August 1997. The officers at D Division Staffing Office were willing to send me to another division if I fit the medical profile for the job, and give me a rank reduction. I considered this to be unfair. Other officers did not have to move or change their rank in similar situations. A rank reduction would mean lower pay and conversion to Public Service Employee or Civilian Member of the RCMP. To me this was not an option. Back at home I cried, then called my lawyer, Roger, and began my grievance. I went to my family physician, Dr. Carre, who had taken care of my health concerns for many years. He was worried the stress of the possible Medical Discharge was hurting me and I should be on medical or stress leave .

The RCMP of D Division did not like the fact I had the nerve to question their decisions. The Division Reps would not help in my preparation of the grievance, which is normally part of their job.

While I was on stress leave, many documents were either sent to me, by mail or hand delivered. These documents consisted of the following: letters regarding the grievances I had submitted, letters and my responses to finding a position in D Division, letters as to my medical status and injury. I received phone calls from various RCMP departments asking when I was returning to work and what was the status of the grievance. One day I was followed and stopped on the highway by an officer from Selkirk Highway Patrol who had been asked to hand-deliver a document. I asked why he had not phoned first and met me at the Gimli Detachment parking lot. He simply indicated that the documents had to be hand delivered. Another time Sergeant Medder stopped me as I was coming out of the Post Office, and again outside a church, to serve documents related to my Medical Discharge and grievance. He refused to listen to my request that I be served in a more professional manner, for example, at the police detachment.

In June 1997, during a follow-up appointment, Dr. Carre informed me a retired RCMP officer, Inspector N. Neige, had come to his office inquiring about my mental health, and when would I be off stress leave. Inspector Neige implied to the physician that I should return to duty the next week and if I did not return to work, the RCMP would reduce my pay. Neige asked Dr. Carre not to inform me of the visit. However, Dr. Carre did speak to me of this meeting. He had told me of this police officer asking these questions because Insp. Neige led him to believe he was concerned for my well-being and in a position of authority. I was shocked and in a state of disbelief.

At home that same day I immediately phoned the Division Representative Officer, Sergeant Stan Mandrake, to inquire if there was some investigation going on about me. I relayed the information regarding the retired RCMP officer asking my family physician probing questions about me. Stan said he was surprised and would have to make some inquiries. A few minutes later he called me back to say that "No, there is no investigation." I told him, "I am making a complaint!" I knew that Dr. Carre would be upset about the complaint and subsequent investigation, as he had advised me not to make a fuss. Dr. Carre had previously worked in a country where the police are feared. His impression of this encounter with the RCMP police was one of fear.

Sergeant Kevin Sloan from RCMP Internal Investigations was

appointed to investigate my complaint of the RCMP Internal Investigation. I was asked to give a statement but did not feel comfortable having this officer in my home and chose to give my statement at my lawyer's office. The investigating officer, Sergeant Sloan, simply implied that Inspector Neige was concerned for my welfare and Gimli is a small town where everyone knows everyone else's business. I said, "I hardly know the man, I have never had any relationship that would constitute friendship and he had no right to contact my physician implying he was on official RCMP business." Sergeant Sloan indicated there was no harm and my complaint was dismissed, as I could not prove orders had or had not come from D Division. Dr. Carre was intimidated by Sergeant Mandrake and denied any information was exchanged. Sergeant Mandrake also indicated nothing could be done against Neige as he was already retired. To this day, I do not know how Inspector Neige found out I was a patient of Dr. Carre or who sent him to gather information.

I began to feel intimidated by the RCMP. I believed if the RCMP could get to my doctor, where would I feel secure? It seemed that every time I stood up to the harassment and abuse, D Division struck me down. Over time this can be emotionally draining. Eventually I sent a letter asking Sergeant Medder not to serve me with documents in public, as it was unprofessional and humiliating. The officers from Administration and Personnel sent a letter agreeing with Sergeant Medder of Gimli, denying me access to the office.

I began to recognize a repeating pattern of my history with the RCMP in Tisdale. My initial reaction was "Oh no, not this abuse again!"

The officers I had worked with at Selkirk, as well as officers from D Division made no effort to inquire about my health. I felt very isolated. In 1997, a new RCMP Health Services Officer was hired, Dr. Tippin. Upon reading my medical file, he noticed I had been on stress leave for a few months with no further contact from D Division. His concern was I might commit suicide. I was surprised and pleased by his call. However, I indicated I did not give any information over the phone to someone I did not know. I asked for a letter to be sent so that I could be assured he was a doctor and not another RCMP officer fishing for private personal information. He agreed to send the letter and I assured him I would not blow my head off. Besides, my weapon was stored at the Selkirk Detachment, secured in my private locker.

Over the years there is a history of RCMP officers who have committed suicide. It is devastating news to hear of such despair and many of these officers have used their own service weapon. It is tragic to know a fellow officer has felt so hopeless that killing himself of herself appears to be the only option. Several years ago, within a six-week period, three RCMP officers committed suicide with their own weapons. This was a devastating blow for my friend John French, who knew one of the officers personally. He called me the day it was announced in our RCMP internet newsletter. I think John was shocked by the fact his friend, who had a strong personality, could be susceptible to depression and suicide. I think John doubted his own strength after that.

There are guidelines and policies within the RCMP for officers who require support with the stress of police work. However, within the RCMP, there are discrimination, inequality and other abuses that send some officers into despair, hopelessness and suicide. To appear weak is the last thing a police officer wants. The services provided by the RCMP do not allow an officer the safety of admitting any type of depression or mental illness: this would be viewed as weak.

During my first year in the RCMP, there was a report of a female RCMP officer shooting herself in the head as she spoke with her ex-husband on the phone. They were in a custody battle over their child. I listened to the men in Tisdale Detachment call her down for being a coward. I did not agree with their interpretation and felt immense sorrow. Depression and mental illness are deadly experiences, ones which I had yet to explore. (…back to my fight….)

My Therapist,
My Savior, Myself

ONE HAS TO ASK 'HOW DO I SURVIVE IN A TOXIC WORK environment?' As I maintained contact with my therapist over the years I learned: to value myself, be accountable for my behaviour and choices, and over time to accept what had happened to me and so let go of the shame and guilt. I came to realize that it was important to deal with the pain and move forward. I faced my past to change my future. My therapist went to great lengths and it took many sessions to get to the root of my shame and hurt. I learned how to recognize a feeling and dig deeper into its real cause. I learned coping skills and relaxation breathing and body work. Body work is where a person gives positive messages to the part of the body that is hurt or unwell in order to heal it. For me it was my injured shoulder. I was confident I had done a good job in blocking out the memory of being raped, however my therapist made me remember every detail so I would be able to let go of the indignity, guilt and blame. I came to realize it was important for me to be able to actually say the words, rape is rape; no consent equals rape and it does not matter how much a person has had to drink, no still means no. Larry G. knew I was not interested in him, and he was only interested in satisfying his own ego. The first time I said 'rape' out loud, I was shocked by the very word, and the impact it had on me, similar to a glass of cold water in the face.

My therapist's gentle probing allowed me to feel safe enough to say anything because I knew she did not judge me. I could swear as much as I wanted to and she never gave me any reason to think she was uncomfortable with the language or topic. I could speak freely, knowing that no matter what I said, she would not criticize me. One cannot risk opening up to a family member or friend as there is the chance they would not be able to handle what is said and might possibly give advice that is not wanted.

No Support From Within
The RCMP

ON SEPTEMBER 8, 1997 I FORWARDED MY GRIEVANCE against the Medical Discharge. Dr. Tippin, RCMP Health Services Service Officer of D Division, had requested a medical assessment of my capabilities and the extent of my injury. Tippin's report of December 1997 indicated there were alternative duties I was fit to perform at that time, and would the RCMP find a position to fit my medical profile? However, Inspector Embrouille, did not think with the same progressive outlook. He refused to make any effort to locate a job for me and indicated that a proper job search had been done. The Medical Review Board always reviews officers who are injured or on medical leave. If an officer can no longer return to the front lines, then, depending on the rank of the officer, a Medical Discharge process can be the next step. However, I was aware of several officers in D Division who had injuries both on and off duty who had been 'accommodated'. The Medical Review Board did not follow the suggestion from Dr. Tippin to look for an alternative position for a Constable with a disability and therefore, a Medical Discharge was the Medical Review

Board's only option. During 1998, the stress and the harassment increased and continued for the next four years. It seemed every day I had to respond to letters or phone calls from offices at D Division.

Thank God for my lawyer, Mr. Roger Bond. I spent a small fortune on fees and expenses related to my case against the RCMP. Probably Canadians believe that the RCMP upholds the law, lives by their standards of justice and equality for all. If the general public only knew the anguish and psychological trauma suffered by many of the officers, they would be shocked.

As a single parent at that time, I asked my lawyer how to keep the legal fees to a minimum. Roger was understanding and suggested I do the 'grunt work'. I would prepare the letters and /or documents, give him a rough draft and he would do his "lawyer thing." The draft would be sent back to me and I would prepare the final document and forward it. This process saved me thousands of dollars. Roger was fair in his billing practices and I wanted to show my appreciation of his expertise and support: he really appreciated the baking I brought to his office, especially my butter tarts which are legendary around town in Gimli.

Baking is a dying art but I find it relaxing. My grandmother, Isabella Ayers, had taught me to bake when I was twelve years old. My first butter tarts had pastry so tough they required a knife to cut them. However, with time, practice and patience from my loving grandmother, I now make pastry that falls into tasty flakes in one's mouth. At every family function I am asked to bring butter tarts. One day when at age fifteen, my grandmother came to me and gave me a wooden spoon. She said as I had surpassed her ability in tart making, she was passing on the torch. From that day forward, I baked the tarts and she baked the pies. I always enjoy giving my baking away.

In 1999, I really had three grievances going at the same time: one against the Medical Discharge, another for failure to identify a suitable position, and a third for the Income Tax and Duty related Injury Adjustment. If an officer is injured in the line of duty and off work for any length of time, they are entitled to reimbursement of the taxes that they have paid on their income. For me, this was a huge chunk of change. I received this adjustment in 1994 to 1996 during my injury and subsequent two surgeries and recovery. However, once I sent in my grievance against the Medical Discharge, the officers in D Division had an attitude change and I was refused the Income Tax Adjustment. The reason behind the refusal was, in my opinion, subjective on their part. I had been off duty with stress leave related to my possible Medical Discharge. The officers claimed my stress leave was not duty related, which I thought was truly vengeful and petty. The entire six year situation could have been avoided had the officers in Staffing and Administration Section used creative thinking in coming up with solutions to keep injured officers, not how to discharge them. This I thought was mental abuse on their part: what other reason would I have had to go on stress leave? My shooting accident and subsequent shoulder injury were the cause of the impending Medical Discharge. Had I not been hurt, I would not be under the threat of termination, and I did not have sufficient years in the Force to qualify for a pension.

By June of 1998, I concluded my grievances and Medical Discharge file were getting bounced from office to office, with each RCMP officer who handled them unwilling to make a decision as what to do; they were probably afraid of setting any type of precedent. On many occasions I would receive letters asking about issues which had already been addressed by another officer in the same office. I wondered what was going on if this type of confusion was occurring in the same office, but I did not give up.

While I was on stress leave, the RCMP had less power over me. During this time, I received numerous letters asking me if I was willing to return to full operational duties. I knew that my injury not only affected my physical ability but also my psychological ability to function adequately. At 5' 6' and just under 135 pounds, not a big police officer, and prior to my injury I never doubted my ability to take someone down. However, with the injury and surgeries, I did have my doubts. I was afraid I might feel pressure to use 'deadly force' where physical restraint would have been appropriate. It was exhausting to receive letters which stated contradictory information about my injury. I followed my surgeon's recommendation that I should not be put in a situation where physical restraint could be required. There was no way I should ever be exposed to any physical resistance in dealing with suspects, and I was not about to take advice from non-medical personnel.

In February 1998 a letter was sent from the RCMP D Division indicating that perhaps I was 'not completely accurate in my claim of mileage to and from physiotherapy appointments. My honesty was being questioned regarding the accuracy of the mileage I was claiming to get to and from physiotherapy appointments. I was entitled to claim mileage for driving to my physiotherapy appointments at a clinic in Winnipeg, Manitoba, from my home in Winnipeg Beach. This is approximately 160 kilometres for the return trip. Following my first surgery, I was unable to drive and had family members drive me to the appointments. Once I was able to handle the car, I drove three times a week to these appointments. Instead of asking about the mileage, they assumed I was committing fraud. I was furious. This was nice way of calling me a liar. I had checked my car and there was an error, but it was determined to be in the trip-meter. I offered to repay the difference if required. I asked, "Why did they take over a year for you to tell me of the error?"

I sent a letter immediately, challenging the comments and explained the difference in the number of kilometres. That was the end of that issue. Nevertheless, it added to my torment, as I had to go through the grieving process. No only for my body injury but for the job I could no longer perform. It was like part of me had died. A huge loss. With the help of my therapist, I was able to recognize I was grieving. I also had a great deal of unidentified anger and had been unaware of the reasons for it. I learned to 'self-talk' to my injury and forgive my body for letting me down in not healing perfectly. 'Self-talk' like body work uses positive words to talk to yourself and find peace and strength. For example, I would find five words to describe myself such as gentle, smart, wanted, fun and loveable.

The RCMP did not share my grief and clearly determined to remove me from the organization by whatever means possible. Little did the RCMP know I was determined to have a fair deal and I would eventually outlive some of these officers who had retired or died during the long process.

However, Inspector Lucy Yorrn, Officer in Charge of Staffing at D Division, put pressure on me to return to operational duties. In her staffing interview with me and the subsequent report submitted, December 30, 1997, she suggested I get re-assessed by the new HSO (Health Service Officer) Dr. Jupe, to determine if I could return to the field with some consideration for my shoulder. She wanted me return to working in the police car. After several letters between Yorrn's office and my lawyer's office she dropped this idea. Inspector Yorrn took a new approach in June 1998. She requested we meet at her office in D Division to discuss a possible job opportunity. I did not feel completely comfortable going alone so I attended the meeting on July 23, 1998, with my daughter's father, John French, who was an active member of the RCMP. He and I had once lived as husband and wife but now, as friends, we had a closer and more understanding relationship. He can depend on me for support and I get the same consideration from him. He was more than happy to come and watch my back.

At the meeting, Insp. Yorrn promised me a job to fit my profile in Selkirk Sub Division and suggested I could start within a few weeks. I was very excited to return to work and be a fully productive officer. But this was about to blow up in my face. I responded to her written offer of the position, July 28, 1998, and advised her I would seek confirmation from my health care providers to ensure my medical profile was updated. I would start work at the Selkirk Sub Division detach-ment on August 10, 1998.

At this time Level l of the grievance against the inadequate job search was accepted to go to the next level. My lawyer requested the Medical Discharge process be held in abeyance pending the decision for Level ll. This was extremely frustrating, as I had received no sup-port during all the years of harassment and unequal treatment. I was completely on my own.

A friend in the RCMP, (who wishes to remain anonymous) told me no one in the history of the RCMP has pursued a grievance against the Medical Discharge and taken the process as far as I have done. I found those words disappointing yet encouraging. I was not about to sail away into the sunset without a fight.

Three Days Of
Humiliation And Despair

I WAS ELATED AT THE PROSPECT OF GOING TO WORK again after all the months of frustration from not working at the job I had enjoyed so much. Desperately I wanted to continue to be a productive officer with the RCMP and felt I was too young to be retired. Feeling confident, I believed the Medical Discharge process would be dismissed and I would be allowed to continue with the RCMP for years.

The night before I was to go to work, I was nervous and yet excited at the prospect of working again. Anxious because I knew I would eventually collide with Larry G., who had raped me. He would be at one of the various coffee shops or at my new office. This thought filled me with fear at my possible reaction to seeing him. My ongoing therapy and inner strength had allowed me to learn not to hold onto the shame. Releasing the pain was going to take time. During the night, I concentrated on taking back my power, believing in myself to handle anything and became secure on this issue. I knew I would overcome this obstacle but letting go of the shame would take many years.

I arrived on time, 08:30 hours, at the Selkirk Sub Division, in my freshly pressed RCMP uniform, minus the gun and bulletproof vest. I actually had some shape, like a woman. I met the two General Investigation Section officers and the secretary who decided to go for coffee upon my arrival. Of course who else from Selkirk Rural Detachment met us at the golf course coffee shop? Yes, it was Larry, sitting among respected officers. He did not look at me. I felt so dirty and unimportant I wanted to disappear but I held my head up with courage, walked by his chair and sat down, making sure he would not be in my line of vision. I was proud of the nerve I had that he could no longer negate. I was thankful not many people talked to me. Being the centre of attention terrified me and having Larry look at me, left a disgusting taste in my mouth. Fortunately, the coffee break was short.

My first day was uneventful. The basement offices had several rooms, with cement walls and floor. The Dog Section also had a room at the end of the hall. This section included a highly trained police dog which is capable of sniffing out drugs, lost people, dead bodies and explosives. The dog has one master, and together they go on all kinds of calls. I worked with the secretary for the Sub Division office. I asked her questions about work opportunities, officers on office and light duties and about what was available for injured RCMP officers and the 'A250 program'. This is a program for which officers are reimbursed for successfully completing courses at University or College. I inquired about university or college courses I may be interested in taking since I was unsure as to my eligibility. She advised me if an officer is on light duties, they are not eligible for the A250 program or payment for courses. So I thought I would take courses at my own expense.

There appeared to be a lack of jobs for me at the Sub Division building and I asked the other officers if they needed any assistance. Unfortunately, their office was quiet at that time and there were no big cases to work on. I would not be able to go out on call with them anyway, due to my medical restriction so I was assigned to shred top secret documents. I was in the main office of Superintendent Kline who, along with his personal secretary and the section Non Commissioned Officer (NCO) Sergeant V. Moyen, were on holidays. I was alone with the radio and the shredder. I turned on the radio, country (not my favorite) and began to shred the boxes of documents stacked up beside the shredder. The boxes resembled the Great Wall of China. I hoped that I would not have to do this for too long. The first day monotonous, long and boring.

I left at end of my shift, 16:30 hours, and headed home with hopes that tomorrow would be more challenging. But I was wrong. The next few days were just as boring as the first. The highlight of each day was going for coffee in the morning to a coffee shop in Selkirk. Lunch was in the office lunchroom and afternoon coffee was either at the office or again in Selkirk. The first week was as dull as powder however I kept hoping with the return of Superintendent Kline, I would be assigned more meaningful duties. Wrong again.

Superintendent Kline returned on Monday, August 17, 1998. I had hoped, with the boss back, there would be interesting duties for me. I came to work eager and ready for a new challenge instead of the shedder. He dropped the bomb on me when he asked "Why are you here? I told Inspector Yorrn not to send you here as there is no work for you to do. I think you are being used as a pawn."

I was crushed and humiliated. The secretary was aware I was not supposed to be at Sub Division but she had not told me. To make matters worse, Superintendent Kline assigned me to Selkirk Rural detachment to be an assistant to the secretaries. This was beyond belief. I was upset and stunned and left his office completely shattered.

Working at the Rural Detachment and possibly having to work with Larry G., was something I could not do. In the evening after a lengthy talk with my therapist, I convinced myself I could do it, or at least try. I got up the next day and went to work at my old detachment.

However, as soon as I walked in, I could feel the dread begin in my feet and quickly move up to my chest, the tightness of fear. Working here was not going to be good for me. Almost immediately I was assigned the jobs the secretaries don't like, for example, doing computer audits on old cases to determine if these files had been correctly submitted. As these duties did not reflect any of my strengths or capabilities, I prepared a letter indicating I am not going to be used as a pawn and promptly left the building. I put the letter on the desk of Sergeant Lavin, the NCO of the detachment, and sent copies to Superintendent Kline and my lawyer. I drove home in tears, scarcely able to breathe from the deep sobs. How could this happen? Who was in charge? What did I do to deserve such humiliating treatment?

I forwarded a complaint against Inspector Yorrn, August 20, 1998, to D Division, for her unprofessional behavior and her failure to keep with the RCMP's Mission, Vision and Value with respect to its stated commitment to the officers. I went to see my doctor and relayed the entire situation. He was sympathetic to my plight and I was put back on stress leave and this is where I stayed.

My surgeon, Dr. DeComby, was contacted again in April 1998 from Dr. Tippin, Health Service Office of D Division, inquiring if my shoulder injury had improved. I think the RCMP had hoped I would be able to perform uniform duties, back in the field. Dr. Tippin knew of my fear of being less than able to protect myself, so to send me back to detachment work and shift work would be a punishment.

D Division had a new Commanding Officer, Assistant Commissioner Featherstone, who took command of the RCMP officers of D Division in May 1998. He would eventually reveal his true colours in how he treated his fellow officers, especially those below his rank, as less than a valued resource. For example, I was aware that in order to be a more marketable officer, I needed to be in a higher rank and felt tremendous pressure to write and pass the Corporal exam. If I passed, I would be promoted and there were more opportunities at this level for an officer with medical restrictions. In addition, I probably would not be faced with a Medical Discharge.

By accident during a conversation with John I found out that all senior Constables who writes the Corporal's exam, would be entitled to a pay raise. I could write the exam, pass, and find a position within the RCMP at a higher rank in a non- operational position. The deadline to apply was April 30, 2000 and I had received this information April 27th. I faxed my request to Sergeant Sinoffski in Staffing.

On May 9, 2000 I called the D Division Representative Sergeant Craig Noman to inquire about writing the Corporal's exam on the next available date, which was May 13th. After several attempts to locate him on May 9th, I managed to speak with him the next day. He advised that after speaking to Sergeant Fauxl, I was not allowed to participate in the exam process until my grievance for the Medical Discharge was settled in my favour. They considered me medically discharged. I immediately called my lawyer.

I was so angry on the following day I called Sergeant Fauxl who further advised me the decision came from Commanding Officer Featherstone. I called Commanding Officer Featherstone. Point blank he told me, "According to me, you are no longer a member of the RCMP even if your grievance is being held in abeyance, therefore you are not eligible to participate in the promotion process." Needless to say this was shocking to hear from the Commander of D Division. How could he refuse my request so coldly, over the phone and not be willing to hear all the facts? I will never know. I took notes of this conversation and documented his response. Making notes was never my strong point during my policing career, but I have since learned the value of good notes. I felt this was necessary to survive the ordeal of an impending Medical Discharge and loss of my financial future. My experience from Tisdale, and the torment and abuse suffered at the hands of a few officers, were always present in my memory. I had to wait for the next kick which would come in the form of phone calls, service of documents in public, denial of grievances, or refusal to accommodate

I continued with the grievances for the Income Tax Adjustment and the Force's failure to do an adequate job search for me across Canada. Our grievance process at that time involved over 30 different stages. I always felt under the gun to respond quickly and get my documents forwarded within the allowed time-frame. D Division, however, requested time extensions in an effort to wear down my resolution in the hopes I would quit and go away. My persistence for justice, fair and equal treatment would not allow me to do this. I had to remind myself I did nothing wrong.

A letter was sent to Commissioner Jones, the "top cop" of the RCMP, to plead my case. There is tremendous power in the rank of Commissioner of the RCMP in Ottawa. He has the authority to order a position be found for an officer. In June 1998, my letter was sent outlining the permanent injury to my shoulder, the subsequent pathetic effort to find a non-operational job for me and the subtle threat of a Medical Discharge if I did not return and resume the position of a front line police officer. No response was ever received from the Commissioner

It seemed my fate was sealed. No one in the RCMP was willing to help.

This Mountie Got Her Man

WITH THE STRESS AND STRAIN OF FIGHTING THE MEDICAL Discharge, there was not much time left for me to date. Also, as a single mother, I wanted to set a good example for my daughter on the issues of relationships and sex.

I had many first dates, dinners, movies and walks in the parks. There is excitement in a first date and getting to know someone for the first time. It seemed once the topic came around to employment and questions about what I did for a living, the men became visibly uncomfortable. For example, I was having dinner one night at a romantic restaurant, in Winnipeg, with a very attractive man. It had been a blind date but I thought, 'I think I lucked out this time, he's a cutie, with nice teeth.'

Dinner was great, with nice wine and candles. Eventually he got to the point where I had to answer the question about my employment. I looked him straight in the face and casually said; "I work for the federal government in the public relations department." I had smiled so sweetly. He asked "Which department?" Reluctantly, I admitted, "Actually, I work for the RCMP." He still was not sure which department in the RCMP. "Oh so you are a secretary." Boldly I added, "I work as a police officer in the RCMP, I am a police officer with Selkirk Highway Patrol." I straightened my shoulders with pride.

His reaction to this was immediate. Shifting in his seat and looking at his plate, then his watch, he said, "Well, I think we should go, I have to work early. It was nice meeting you." This is code for 'I am out of here'. I left without having dessert. Eventually, I would tell prospective dates about my job just see their reaction. Of the few men who were impressed with my position of authority, was David, who ultimately became my husband. We met in Winnipeg at physiotherapy in August of 1995 and began dating in March 1996. He thought my being a female officer was great and he liked my independent spirit, something the women in his past did not possess.

I had great support from David during the years of the grievances and Medical Discharge. In February 1999 Dr. Tippin called me to advise me there would be a medical review of my case and indicated he was aware that Staffing and Personnel from D Division would not make the effort to notify me of the meeting. Dr. Tippin, felt I should be made aware of what was happening. I thanked him.

I sent a letter to Staffing and Personnel asking for an explanation as to why no effort had been made to notify me of the medical review. Once again papers began to fly. Staffing forwarded a response that the reason for the delay in the second job search was due to: insufficient documentation regarding my permanent disability, and the holdup in receiving documentation from my surgeon. Inspector Yorrn sent another letter a few days later explaining that the medical review did not necessarily mean the officer would be subjected to a Medical Discharge. Is this hope?

On May 3, 1999, as I came out of the Gimli Lutheran Church, I was approached by Sergeant Medder and served Notice of Medical Discharge papers. The documents included were from Dr. Tippin confirming my permanent injury would not allow me to return to operational police duties. There was also a letter from Inspector Yorrn, advising me the second job search across Canada had not been successful in locating a suitable position.

I was very angry at being served in public and promptly faxed a copy of the notice to my lawyer, Roger Bond. I had to appoint a doctor to act on my behalf to the Medical Board Appointment, so I asked Dr. DeComby, my surgeon. The review board had in fact, agreed that my injury was permanent and a Medical Discharge was the only option available. The doctors involved were never given any other "accommodation" option.

Being stuck in this oppressive state for so many months began to take its toll on me physically. I had been having severe pain in my upper gastric area and intestines, a problem which had been plaguing me for months. I had seen my local doctor who had suggested it could be Irritable Bowel Syndrome and to eat more fibre. As it turned out, more fibre nearly killed me and the symptoms got worse. I lost weight and became very thin. I was referred to a gastrointestinal specialist, Dr. Roland Galardy, who requested that tests be done. As a result, he was able to determine that my illness was Celiac Disease, an allergy to gluten. Severe stress can bring on the symptoms. There was no question as to where this anxiety came from.

I remember the day when Dr. Galardy told me the news of my illness. I had brought some home baked cookies to his office for my follow up appointment. He told me that I had Celiac Disease, and explained what it is, and how a complete change in my diet would improve my health. I was devastated. I had never had to worry about food and ate everything, except peas. Now I had to worry about the flours, spices, and other additives. I felt lost with no life raft in sight. After leaving the doctor's office I went to meet David for lunch. He was working for the Winnipeg City Parks and Recreation department doing maintenance and upkeep of City lawns and parks. I drove to the location where he was working and when I came to where he usually parked his tractor, he was not in sight. I left him a note saying, 'David, got bad news from doctor, scared, very terrible, meet me at the bagel shop.'

I did not realize what an impact these words would have on David. He drove up on the tractor a few minutes later and came, running to the bagel shop. I was sitting by the window watching him and thought, 'Oh, maybe he only has few minutes for lunch.' He came in with a very concerned look on his face and he was frowning. I started to cry when he walked up to me and just pulled me into his arms and said gently, "Oh sweetie, everything will be okay."

I told him what the doctor had said about having Celiac disease and how this would affect me forever. He was so relieved, "Oh, is that all?" He had gotten my message, and his interpretation was I was dying of cancer. Then he got angry about the note and I promised never to leave a cryptic message like that again. David was always supportive and within several months, we would be engaged.

I was determined to overcome this obstacle. Eventually I created my own recipes, which are delicious. Once I purchased a bread maker, began making my own bread, buns, pizza and other dough products. When I realized how many people had Celiac Disease, and the dearth of available food substitutes at the time, I decided to make my disease an opportunity and within a couple of months, created my own part time business selling Gluten Free baked goods, calling it Sherry's "Love to Bake."

In the spring of 1999 a flurry of paperwork bounced back and forth among me, Roger's office and various offices at D Division regarding my grievance on being discharged.

"….. But Officer…"

A police officer is fortunate to be privy to some sensitive situations, many of which can be quite funny. During my police career, I tried to balance the good and the bad. For example, one sunny afternoon while on Highway 8 north of Selkirk, Manitoba, I was alone in the police car, on patrol and running radar. Enforcing speed limits consists of running and stationary radar. Running radar occurs when the police car is driving the speed limit with the radar beam turned on and facing oncoming traffic, there is a set speed at which the radar machine gives a ringing sound when an approaching vehicle is traveling higher than the set speed.

It appeared I was the only vehicle on the road and had assumed it would be a slow day. While I was admiring the fields of golden wheat I drove north on one of the major highways, when suddenly the radar began to make the ringing sound and a southbound car, came zooming into the radar beam. I watched the flash of the silver car whiz by me. I immediately activated the dome lights on the roof of the car, flipped the wigwag headlights on and aggressively turned around in pursuit.

I followed at about 120 Kilometres for a few minutes and car did not appear to be slowing down. I thought perhaps this could be a stolen vehicle or an impaired driver not wanting to get charged. The lights were going, the siren was blaring and the driver refused to stop. I was getting angry. I pulled up along side the car and motioned to the driver to pull over on right shoulder. She looked at me with a distressed face. I slowed my vehicle to drop in behind her car. Finally, the vehicle's signal light came on indicating the car was pulling to the right shoulder. The car slowed and came to a stop. I called in my location and got out. I was feeling irritated at the dangerous speed this car was going and wondered why the driver had not stopped when I was behind the car. I approached the lone female occupant who had a panicked look on her face. My initial reaction was to give her a ticket but her story was believable.

"Oh officer, thank God, sorry I couldn't stop because you see, I have diarrhea and my house is right there. I was coming from my friends and suddenly had to go! Sorry." She was pointing to a driveway along the highway a few hundred yards south, her face showing concern for her ability to make the driveway and prevent an internal explosion.

My attitude changed as I could relate to her predicament. "Next time don't drive so fast, it is dangerous." I let her continue on her way. She was very relieved and drove to her home. I watched from my car as she came to an abrupt stop, threw open the driver's side car door and raced into the house, leaving the outside door swinging in the wind. I had to laugh. During my service in the RCMP of all the tickets that I had issued, she had a believable and understandable excuse not to get a ticket.

Another interesting experience occurred on a cold windy night during the summer of 1994. Again, I was alone in the police car, patrolling up and down Highway 8. I noticed a car with one headlight out, approaching southbound. I activated my police lights and proceeded to turn around to follow. The vehicle stopped immediately and before I could call my location and the vehicle plate number on the radio, the driver got out of the car. I tossed the radio receiver in the air and quickly opened my door as the male driver walked swiftly towards my side of the police car. The wind was howling across the highway. The driver kept coming toward me. I started to sweat, my life was moving in slow motion. Fear was building. I yelled at him to "Stop!" "Stop!" "Stop!" He kept moving toward me. I saw him reach into the right side of his coat and pull out something black with silver. I thought, "Oh my God, he has a gun!" I yelled again for him to "Stop!" I dropped to one knee, using the car door as a shield leaned to the left with only my hands showing, and pointed my gun straight at him. I waited to see his gun point at me before I shot him. I can remember the sound of my heart pounding louder than the wind that was shaking the car. Or perhaps my terror of getting killed was causing the world to tremble around me. I reacted the way I was taught, take cover and draw your weapon. In the split second I had observed him reaching for something from inside his coat, I pulled my gun from the safety of the holster. Now I was armed and ready to blow him away. While I was focusing on his hand movements, his shiny belt buckle sparkled in the flashing lights. I yelled again "Stop where you are!" He continued to move forward until he looked up at me and suddenly became aware of what was happening. He saw my gun pointed at him and realized what I was yelling. He stopped less than three feet from me, staring like a deer in the beam of my headlights. His mouth dropped open and he was speechless. Now it was his turn to focus on my gun pointing chest height at him. He stopped dead in his tracks with the wallet hanging limply in his left hand. It was a long black wallet with silver chain attached. For a few seconds the world seemed to stop and we stared at each other, both of us realizing what could have happened.

I broke the silence, "I told you to stop, why didn't you listen? I could have shot you! Next time you are stopped by the police stay in your vehicle. If you were in the States, they would have blown you away! Get back to your car." I felt my anger was justified. I nearly shot him and I would have done it instinctively. He stood frozen while I holstered my gun and walked towards him. I ushered him to his car and told him to "stay put." I don't think he moved a muscle for ten minutes. Fear is a strange experience: people never really know how they will react to a life or death situation until faced with the decision.

My training to react to this type of situation had been successful. I was taught to shoot if I saw a weapon or a gun. I had to wait those few seconds as the wallet was being pulled from his coat to confirm whether or not he had a gun. It was important my eyes did not lie to me but see the reality. Most officers don't have a few seconds to react and find cover. I was lucky. I didn't give him a ticket, just a warning to get the headlight fixed. I figured that he probably had enough of a scare, just like I did. I can still see his shiny belt buckle. As he drove away, I pulled onto the shoulder of the road and sat there for a few minutes thinking how both our lives could have changed forever in those few seconds. I thought of Nadine: what would she think if I had killed someone? What would have happened to me if I had mistakenly shot and killed a man because I thought he had a gun? These questions were on my mind every day while I was on duty. Despite this trepidation, my motto during my service was that it is better to be judged by twelve than carried by six, and no one was going to raise my daughter but me. This determination to survive enabled me to find strength in all aspects of my life.

Back In The Battle
And Justice For All

LIKE MENTIONED PREVIOUSLY, THE WAR OF WORDS between me and the RCMP of Winnipeg D Division picked up speed during 1999. It seemed every other day I was preparing some letter or response relating to the Medical Discharge against me, the grievance regarding the Canada-wide job search, the complaint of harassment and intimidation by Inspector Neige (Rtd.) and Inspector Yorrn, the unprofessional behavior of Sergeant Medder and the two Income Tax grievances. What else could the RCMP do to me, take away my birthday?

Daily life consisted of driving Nadine to school in the morning, then going to the library to prepare a letters. Summer came and went and as fall approached the phone calls and letters from D Division arrived more frequently. The calls from the Gimli Detachment to pick up documents became a regular nuisance. I found the drive to the Gimli Detachment and being served documents extremely stressful. My breathing became shallow and the palms of my hands were sweaty. I wore sunglasses so no one in the office would see the panic on my face. In Manitoba we have a winter with many sunny days so I did not look foolish wearing sunglasses. I did not realize this was a panic attack, something I had never experienced before. After contacting my therapist to discuss the situation with the ongoing grievance process, I asked her what could be happening to me. My therapist and I worked on what to do whenever I felt under extreme stress and a panic attack coming.

I was to do deep breathing to calm myself down and focus on the task. At first it was difficult to calm down under the constant stress of possibly losing my job with the RCMP. However, after practicing this technique several times I was eventually able to go to the Gimli Detachment without wearing my sunglasses and without having a panic attack.

Although my life seemed turned upside down with the RCMP, it was important to find happiness wherever possible. Exercise, baking and spending time with Nadine and David were part of my self-care. David and I were engaged on August 28, 1999. He took me on a hike to Whiteshell Provincial Park, hid the ring by a spruce tree and proposed to me under the tree. It was romantic and intimate. Getting engaged to a wonderful and caring man was truly a blessing. We began to plan our wedding for April 15, 2000. As for my money situation, I continued to hope the grievance decision would be in my favour and I could continue on to a rewarding career in the RCMP. This was not to be. As fall approached, no news was not good news. My birthday drew near and my gift from the RCMP was a phone call advising that documents were sent to the Gimli Detachment to be served on me – Notice of Discharge.

Two days later on November 3, 1999 I was served my Notice of Discharge document to be effective December 1, 1999. Which meant in thirty days I had to return to the Gimli Detachment to be medically discharged. I was humiliated at being served my discharge papers by Sergeant Medder, the same man against whom I had made a complaint for his unprofessional conduct in serving documents on me in public. The Cheshire cat grin on his face made my blood boil. I never thought the day would come when the actual Medical Discharge would be successful, and I had remained hopeful. He demanded that my badge and all my uniforms must be returned upon the discharge date. I was devastated. All my efforts of trying to remain in the RCMP seemed to come unraveled in one full swoop! However, I managed to maintain my dignity, sign for the paper and leave the Detachment with my head held high.

This was not over, not by a long shot. I came home and packed up all my old uniforms in a garbage bag, squeezed in my RCMP ceremonial dress uniform, the red serge, old work boots, old uniform shirts and pants. I left the bag in the bedroom in the corner, to be returned to the RCMP in less than a month. All the symbols of my past and future career were in that bag. The contents sat silent in the corner, along with my hopes and dreams. I cried at the thought of the injustice of it all. I had done nothing wrong and yet was I being punished for insisting on equal treatment.

The Notice of Discharge document indicated I was "medically and mentally" unable to return to full operational duties. I sent a letter asking for the "mental disability" to be removed, as being stressed is not considered a "mental disability." I received a letter from Sergeant Jake Fauxl, on December 3, 1999, who was in charge of the grievance section at D Division. He refused to remove the words mental disability and as if to reassure me added the reasons for discharge would not be made public except with my consent. In his opinion my disability was both physical and mental. The issue of the wording of mental disability was addressed with the RCMP Health Services Officer, Dr. Jupe, who suggested that I could always grieve the wording and have it removed or changed. When did 'stress leave' become a disability? I knew once the constant worry of losing my job, the phone calls, documents being served on me in public places, and massive amounts of paper work were eliminated, there would no be severe stress.

The three weeks leading up to the dismissal date left me an emotional wreck. Questions were nagging me as to how I would pay for Nadine's music lessons, school trips, clothes, the mortgage and household expenses. I remembered my struggle to get off welfare, being a single parent with no money or education, and wanting to provide a good home for Nadine. Joining the RCMP had given me the opportunity to offer her a better life and the financial freedom that comes with a secure and regular income. The overwhelming fear of losing my job and the economic stability which it had provided gripped me. The very thought of being poor again was terrifying. Although David had employment, it was seasonal part-time income and was not sufficient to pay the bills, so he took a full-time job at a hotel in Winnipeg as a security officer, working night shifts.

One thing I was thankful for was the fact I had renewed my mortgage at a much lower rate and over a longer period. I had done this with the logical thought of a worst-case scenario regarding the outcome of the Medical Discharge grievance. I needed payments, which were manageable on a lower income.

David and I scrambled with our finances. The pay at the hotel was just over minimum wage, and one of us needed to be working. Our wedding planned for April 15, 2000, but with my financial future so precarious and with no money coming in, I wanted to postpone the date. David said, "No way am I letting the RCMP force us to change our wedding. We will manage to pay for it."

The thirty days ended. Again, I was called to the Gimli Detachment in order to be served the discharge papers and turn in my badge. I tried to remain optimistic despite the fear of no money was a heavy weight on my shoulders. The bag of my uniforms was put in the car and I drove to the Gimli Detachment. I brought the bag in to the front reception area and told the secretary, "This is for Sergeant Medder." As I waited, I glanced around and felt a pang of pain knowing this would be the last time I would come to the RCMP detachment as an officer. I studied the missing persons' bulletins on the walls, wondering if I would ever be able to help them. The best part of being a police officer was helping people. The ache in my chest was suffocating and my eyes became blurred. I did not want to show weakness in front of the staff so I swallowed hard, took a deep breath, reached for a piece of gum and began chewing with great vigor in order to distract my mind from the terrible, emotional burden of handing in my badge. Sergeant Medder was called to the front of the office and I watched as he swaggered toward the reception glass. I hoped that my voice would not betray my emotions and spoke in a clear but emotionless tone as I indicated my uniforms were in the garbage bag. Then he asked for my badge and suggested I could get it encased in resin to keep. As I handed it over, anger swept over me like a tidal wave. I wanted to throw the bag at this man who seemed incapable of showing any compassion as he smiled at me.

My heart was breaking as I let go of the little piece of tin that was once signifying my career and RCMP identification. I began to feel the internal struggle of finding out who I was without the RCMP. The next few minutes were a blur. My mind was not in the moment. I left the office and headed toward my car. Holding back the pain was impossible as I climbed into the driver's seat and drove home to Winnipeg Beach. Those ten miles seemed to take forever. The tears flowed, making it difficult to see the road, and I had to squint several times just to see the centre line. My chest ached from the deep sobs wracking my body. My eyes were swollen and red. Before going into the house, I sat in the car for a few more minutes to regain my composure, I had to remain strong for my daughter, and she needed me. I wiped the tears from my puffy eyes and took a few deep breaths. Had I come into the house crying and falling apart she would be very frightened. Christmas was coming and I was thankful I had bought all my presents in November, although I really did not feel particularly merry. Slowly I got out of the car, closed the garage door, and took a few more deep breaths, letting the cold air fill my lungs. A calm came over me as I focused on the next grievance my lawyer and I would be preparing the next day. A glimmer of hope filtered through as I walked up the porch and into the house. The smells of supper filled my senses; the sound of Nadine practicing on the piano echoed a sense of safety and comfort. Tonight, I would not worry about the future but would simply enjoy being with my family. Later that night while we were in bed, David held me as I cried my eyes out. I let him know of all my fears and the disappointment of having to give up my prospects of a career in the RCMP. I cried for the anger I felt at the injustice of these grievances, the discrimination from D Division and lack of support from the Division Representatives. I cried for my isolation from the very organization I had been so proud to serve. And I cried for myself, for the heavy load I had been carrying for so long. David was wonderful; he did not try to interrupt me as I vented my pain through the tears. Then as I lay exhausted in his arms, he quietly offered suggestions on what to do next and suggested that I take one-step at a time. He was the one person who was able to get me back to thinking logically and to not allow emotion to cloud my judgment in making decisions.

The next day I drove to drive to Winnipeg to see the doctor at Veterans Affairs for my Medical Discharge interview on the status of my duty related injury. I was to receive a small amount of money for the injury. The doctor who examined me indicated that within the next couple of months I would be receiving a monthly payment for my injury.

The next few weeks were stressful as Christmas approached, bills were coming due and David had to work night shifts in Winnipeg to make ends meet. I began to look in the papers for work that fit my experience and interests. However, given my limited education, it was more difficult than I had imagined. I did not want a minimum wage job so I decided to take courses in the Human Resource field.

Like the answer to a prayer, a phone call came from Pay Section at D Division a few days before Christmas, telling me I was 'reinstated in the RCMP', which meant continued pay and full benefits pending the outcome of my grievance. My lawyer had sent in a grievance against the Medical Discharge to Ottawa on December 2, 1999, the day after I dropped my bag of uniforms and badge at Gimli. I was delighted to receive this information and to know the back pay from the beginning of December may take a few weeks to arrive. This was wonderful, the best Christmas present I could have asked for. I thought it might be a joke, but it was not. The fight was on again.

I went to see my lawyer regarding the Notice of Discharge and he informed me of the forwarding the grievances for both the Income Tax Adjustment and Notice of Discharge to Ottawa (which I had started in 1997). This was good news, at least my grievances were moving ahead, and I wondered what the final outcomes would be. Who would be the first to blink in this game of chicken? The RCMP had the money to outlast me, but I had the desire and the driving force within me to seek justice, equal and fair treatment for men and women in the RCMP.

Once I knew that I was reinstated, sent a letter to Sergeant Fauxl in D Division requesting the return of my badge. This little piece of tin was part of my identity and I needed to have it back. The response from Sergeant Fauxl, December 29, 1999, is as follows:

"Your request to have your badge returned, as it is your view that you have been reinstated, cannot be granted at this time. While the discharge process has been suspended pending the outcome of your grievance, your discharge is related to a medical condition which does not allow you to function in the capacity of a police officer. Therefore, there is no requirement for you to have the identification badge at this time. IF at some point, you are able to resume duties as a police officer, your badge will be returned. In the interim, it will be held at this office."

I found this unbelievable. Why would they not return my badge? Did other officers, when off duty sick or pregnant, have to turn in their badge if they went on office duties? No, they did not. So why should I? Once again, this was no equality. Sergeant Fauxl's blatant disregard in returning my badge angered me. I would not give up. I had to pick my battles and the return of the badge was put on the back burner while dealing with the other two grievances. In my mind, I was still an officer with the same rights and I would not allow that be taken away by D Division.

During the previous year I had frequent correspondence sent to Ron Duhamel, a Member of Parliament in Ottawa, who represented St. Boniface in Winnipeg. This had been David's political riding when he lived in Winnipeg. David was invited to the 10th anniversary party for Mr. Duhamel as a Member of Parliament, and he asked me to accompany him. At the gathering I was able to speak privately with Mr. Duhamel, and we discussed the discrimination and unequal treatment within the RCMP. I told him of my work injury and how the RCMP wanted to medically discharge me, while injured male officers were "accommodated." He was intrigued and offered to bring my situation up in Parliament and to speak to the Solicitor General, Laurence MacAulay. He asked a letter outlining my grievance be sent to his constituency office in Winnipeg. History would show he was an honest and caring man.

Speaking to Mr. Duhamel gave me hope again this grievance process could come to a successful conclusion. Shortly after this meeting, I forwarded a letter, together with copies of documents outlining my grievance, to Ron Duhamel's office.

The original response from the Solicitor General went to my lawyer's office and I received a copy of the letter January 7, 2000, saying "the Commissioner of the RCMP deals with management and control of the RCMP, therefore, I should go through the internal process." The letter also suggested that "The RCMP had made many attempts to locate a suitable position for me but, due to my injury being permanent, very unlikely a suitable job would be found."

I was very surprised at the suggestion the RCMP had made 'many attempts to find me a job.' This was a blatant untruth and I had the documents to prove what little effort had been made to locate me a position. In fact, the attempt to locate a position and the RCMP's failure to do so was part of my grievance. The grievance sent forward in 1997 had two issues: the first was that the RCMP of D Division did not perform an adequate Force-wide search; the second was to require an explanation as to why other injured officers were found suitable positions and were allowed to continue with their careers or leave on their own terms. I listed the names of officers I knew in D Division who had been 'accommodated' for non-duty related injuries. Little did I know at this point the struggle would continue for another two and a half years: another two and a half years filled with lies and more lies.

Lies, Lies and More Lies

THERE WAS NOW TENSION AT HOME OVER THE POSSIBILITY of no money and my fight with the RCMP. I was worried about how to pay bills as my pay cheques had not arrived for the first six weeks of 2000 and I had to rely on David's income to help. It was difficult for me to ask him for money as I prided myself on being completely independent. I realized my pride was getting in the way of our relationship and I needed to allow people to help me during this trying time. The grievance against the Medical Discharge was the most important issue as I was trying to maintain my financial future. I was also fighting the discrimination against injured female officers in the RCMP and the favouritism shown towards injured male officers.

It was important not to let the sense of failure take over the need for equality and justice. It was a difficult task to dust myself off and carry on. Each time the RCMP sent letters denying information, access to police detachments, or gave negative feedback, I responded by refusing to be bullied or intimidated. There was a bombardment of paperwork back and forth between my lawyer, Roger and D Division.

Roger commented, "They are trying to get rid of you by death of a thousand cuts. We just have to keep going and eventually someone will see that the RCMP is breaking the Canada Labour Laws."

People I knew would ask me, "Why don't you just quit and move on to another career?" My reply was simple, "I quit, they win. What kind of message am I giving my daughter if I quit every time life gets rough? The RCMP helps the male officers but not the female officers and that is not fair. That is not equality." Usually people got the drift, and if they didn't, this was not my problem.

Although my letter to the Commissioner, which had been sent several months previously, had received a response from the Solicitor General, there was no attempt at a resolution by the RCMP. The Commissioner's office indicated in the letter it would be a conflict of interest if his office intervened as Commissioner Murray would be the adjudicator on the Level ll part of my grievance. Again no help and any contact between the Commissioner and I could affect a decision. This of course did not discourage me at all. I would go onward again to another office in government. I felt my case was being sent from office to office with no one taking responsibility to do something. Anything.

I decided to send a follow-up letter to Member of Parliament, Ron Duhamel. I felt it was important he know the true facts, there had been little or no effort put forth into locating a suitable position for me within the RCMP. The Commissioner informed Ron Duhamel I had been offered a different position in the RCMP. However that letter failed to clarify the offer required a rank reduction from that of a regular officer to civilian, resulting in a substantial reduction in pay and pension. My argument was if the RCMP did not force an injured male officers to take a rank reduction and different job classification, why the hell should I? So I had refused. The letter from the Solicitor General failed to explain these facts to Ron Duhamel.

All during early winter and spring of 2000, letters and phone calls went back and forth among my lawyer, D Division and myself regarding the return of my badge, the grievances and harassing behaviour from Sergeant Medder's repeated unprofessional conduct in serving me confidential documents in public. After being subjected to this public service of documents, I had had enough. I decided to send in a letter of complaint to D Division and to not worry about the consequences.

My complaint against Sgt. Medder for unprofessional behaviour was submitted in early February 2000. He ignored my polite request when I asked him, "please call me to come to the Gimli detachment to get the documents."

Shortly after receiving the letter from the Solicitor General, I called the Gimli detachment to ask for a copy of an RCMP form to submit some papers to D Division. The secretary said I was no longer allowed in the detachment as per Sergeant Medder's orders and I was to have been notified by letter from D Division. I could tell she was embarrassed. She said, "Sorry Sherry but I was told that a letter was sent to you." I was angry and humiliated, my cheeks burned with outrage. It was as if I had done something naughty and was being punished. I thought, 'Am I being made to pay for sending in my grievances, or for standing up for my rights as an officer in the RCMP. Could it be because I am a woman fighting for equality?' I knew this was retribution for sending in a complaint against the Gimli Detachment commander, Sergeant Medder who was now refusing to allow me access to what he called 'his' detachment. I recognized the possible problems of allowing this mistreatment and discrimination to continue and decided to boldly go where no female RCMP officer had gone before.

Later that day I went to the mail and found a letter from Sgt. Jake Fauxl, stating I would not be receiving my badge even though I was not medically discharged and entrance to Gimli Detachment was denied including restricted access to RCMP facilities. If I needed to do research for my grievance, I would have to get permission from the Officer in Charge of the Selkirk Detachment, Insp. Lucy Yorrn. Gimli is ten minutes from my home, and Selkirk is a thirty five-minute drive. That would mean I would have to drive sixty kilometers to a photocopy machine or to send a fax. This made no sense. It also made no sense I would have to get permission from Insp. Yorrn who had, just a year ago, lied to me about a position in Selkirk Sub Division. I had made a complaint against Insp. Yorrn and forwarded it to Commanding Officer Featherstone, D Division. The complaint specified the humiliating treatment to which I had been subjected in going to a job that did not exist, and the attempts made to force me to be an assistant to the detachment secretaries. Now D Division expected me to ask this same Inspector for permission to use the manuals. One can only imagine how accommodating Inspector Yorrn would have been. You have got to keep reading in order to fully understand the RCMP organization.

I kept all correspondence and although I was discouraged, my lawyer said, "Let the RCMP keep shooting themselves in the foot, this is good for us. I know it is hard on you, but hang in there."

As it was, I relied on my friend, the father of my daughter, John French, for assistance in getting information from the manuals, copies of forms and changes in policies for the grievance process. He was a lifesaver in finding information on what was going on in D Division and the RCMP. Although John and I had not been a couple for a good many years, we had become great friends and he became a solid support in my years with the RCMP.

Family and friends would often give me advice and comments like, "Why don't you quit?" "Why not sue them?" "Can't you go to the Canadian Human Rights Commission?" "Why do you want to work for an organization that treats its women so badly?"; "Can't you send a letter to the Commissioner or the papers?" I appreciated their support and concern, however, it was necessary to follow the policies and procedures within the RCMP in forwarding grievances. I could not make a Canadian Human Rights Complaint until I had exhausted all internal processes prior to sending a complaint.

Money was scarce and my pay cheques, which should have been deposited to my account while the grievance process continued, had not arrived. I also did not have any police identification and my RCMP medical number had been cancelled. Therefore, when I went to a doctor or tried to get a prescription, there was no record of me as an active serving officer. I contacted the Health Services office and inquired about the problem and was informed the delay came from the office of Administration and Personnel. The necessary paperwork to have me added back to the system had not been sent. I was again angered but not surprised by these 'delays'. I was unable to make an appointment with specialists as I was not covered by RCMP insurance nor Manitoba Health. This was frustrating and time-consuming in terms of phone calls and letters. I was so embarrassed when filling a prescription at the local pharmacy, and the pharmacist would say, aloud, "The system keeps bouncing back the request for payment". The computer records indicated I had been dismissed and I had to convince the pharmacist that I was not. I felt like my credibility was in question at all times. It was embarrassing having to do this in public, to explain why my regimental number was cancelled and the reason for the delay in getting it back on the system. My explanation was often viewed with skepticism.

While continuing with the grievances and sending letters back and forth on a weekly basis, I was also preparing for my wedding, which was set for April 15, 2000. David and I had decided not to live together until we were married. It was important for me to be married before we lived in the same house. All during the course of our relationship, I was involved in the battle with the RCMP to keep my job. This situation, at times, placed stress on my relationship with David. He was supportive and sometimes a little too wound up regarding my struggle.

In life, we have relationships that come and go and lessons are learned. For a life partner, I wanted a person who had a good sense of humour, was honest, generous, reliable and trustworthy. These were qualities that I valued in myself. With my fear of intimacy stemming from past experiences and relationships, it was important I learn to trust again and feel safe. David allowed me to unlock my soul and share my past pain in the safety of his arms. He never judged me nor made me feel shame for the sexual assaults I had suffered. For this reason, I opened up and allowed myself to be vulnerable. There is pain that comes with taking a chance with love. Being in love does not mean everything is perfect. Far from it. We have had our share of struggles and disappointments, however we continue to use effective communication to strengthen our love. He adores me and I trust him. Within a few months of dating I knew we were compatible.

We decided to have a small wedding and keep expenses down. In Manitoba, couples often have a wedding social in order to raise funds for the wedding reception. This is a dance where the price of the entrance tickets goes to the couple. Our social on April 1, 2000 raised sufficient funds to pay for our wedding reception, and to further cut costs, I made tarts and cookies for the 80 people who were attending. We had chosen to hold the ceremony and reception at Officers Mess Hall at HMCS Chippawa, Naval Reserve, in Winnipeg, where David worked. I tried not to think of the chaos with the RCMP while preparing the room for our wedding, and helping with the table arrangements, but it was always in the back of my mind, like a dark secret gripping my guts tight. This tension was my constant companion for years. However, for a short time, the excitement of the wedding helped keep these feelings from dominating my wedding day.

On April 15, 2000 my daughter and I drove from our home in Winnipeg Beach to Winnipeg, for the wedding. David had stayed in Winnipeg the night before to ensure that any last minute problems could be handled. I had my wedding dress in the back seat along with a picnic of champagne, cheese and crackers for our post-wedding night. As David is an officer in the military we were able to use the Officers Mess free of charge. The tables were set up in rows, with white linen, navy blue napkins and navy blue candles. The head table was decorated with white Christmas lights along a navy blue band with matching bows across the front of the table. Crystal champagne glasses stood, gleaming, on the head table, in the glow of the tiny white lights. I had often heard of people having wedding jitters. I had none. I did not suffer any type of anxiety. There was no second-guessing nor any doubts about getting married, and this surprised me. I believe my sense of calm was due to the fact I had no hesitation as to my love for David and his devotion to me. My gown was a simple white dress with spaghetti straps and beaded chest, and a long train, which could be fastened to the back of the dress for dancing.

After booking into the hotel, Nadine and I changed and drove to the reception. Parking across the street allowed me to stop and wait for traffic to pass and to glance up at the building where today I would become a married woman. Then I got excited. Nadine and I raced up the stairs; I was taking them two at a time with my white pumps and flowing train.

The first person I saw was David, coming out of the Officers' Mess. I was very surprised at how calm my future husband appeared to be. He said it was like preparing for a big game. As Nadine and I stood outside the Officers' Mess, I held her hand and looked at her: "Here we go, sweetie." The wedding song was soft and beautiful. "It Had To Be You" was the song they played as Nadine and I walked into the Officers' Mess holding hands, each carrying a small bouquet of white flowers. I did not look at the guests because I did not want to fall apart in case anyone was crying. David was watching us as we entered, and a hush came over the entire room. My stomach was fluttering, like one feels on a rollercoaster. I took a deep breath and walked up the center of the room between the rows of tables.

The ceremony was short and sweet with Pastor Leslie also with the Naval Reserve officiating. Emotion overcame me as I said my vows, looking into my husband's face. There were no doubts about marrying David. A friend, who was a musician and a professor of music, had offered to play his trumpet and had brought a pianist to accompany him. They played during dinner. The toasts to the bride and groom were funny, not mushy. I gave a toast to Nadine and presented her with a gold locket and said, "To my dear Nadine, no matter who comes into my heart, there is no one who can replace the wonderful love I have for my little girl." There was a collective ' Awwwww' from the guests.

David made a beautiful speech about why he wanted to marry me, and of course I cried. Shortly after the speeches the dancing and the drinking began. I was happy to see John French, Nadine's father, there with his date. I truly wanted him to come to my wedding as he is and will always be an important part of our lives. As I greeted the guests he walked up and gave me a hug: "Way to go Benson, you look marvelous." I started to cry. He referred to me as 'Benson' as a term of affection. It was a lovely day and a lovely night.

David and I did not go on a honeymoon for financial reasons. Gifts and our social money covered the cost of the wedding and we were able to buy a new TV, gas powered grass trimmer and a book on relationships by Dr. Phil. I never cared about making lots of money from the wedding, but I really did not want to go into huge debt. David had been working the night shift at a hotel in Winnipeg, and part time with the Naval Reserve. In May he was to attend Fleet School in Quebec City for a Naval training course for seven weeks.

Shortly after the wedding, the response from Sergeant Fauxl, D Division, on my complaint against Sergeant Medder did not surprise me. The letter justified the serving of private documents in public and my no longer being allowed to use his detachment. Nothing was done to improve Medder's communication abilities or in the service of confidential documents. I received a letter on March 17,

2000 from D Division, Staff/Sergeant Gilroe regarding my complaint against Medder. Again, no fault was found with Sergeant Medder's behaviour, and according to Gilroe, I was being treated like any other person in the general public who required the service of documents. What else could they say? That he was completely wrong? It was the 'old boys club' sticking up for each other. In doing so, they allowed his conduct to continue.

There were many times during the lengthy process I was at my wits' end. Admitting these feelings of being overwhelmed was terrifying. I believed I was a rational person but after being battered for so long, felt my inner strength begin to slip away and I felt hopeless about ever getting my career back on track within the RCMP. I could not always talk to my husband or family as they were not aware of the police culture and procedural steps to be taken in forwarding a grievance. I relied on the clear head and expertise of my therapist from Saskatoon. Regular calls to her kept me sane in coping with the months and months of being bombarded with letters and phone calls. Payment for these sessions was made through Health Services Office. The medical form has parts that need to be completed. I would fill out the patient portion and the doctor-therapist would complete the remainder and mail the form to D Division. The RCMP made it difficult to obtain the various forms required for medical appointments and I was unable to make some appointments with specialists. However, as I had no access to any detachment and D Division refused to send forms, I had no choice but to call the RCMP D Division Psychologist, Dr. Pat Fixet, and explain the situation. He was very understanding, which was a pleasant surprise to me. I had expected resistance from his office as he was working for the very organization trying to fire me. Dr. Fixet said the forms would be sent to me immediately and if there were further problems in getting the proper medical forms, I should contact his office. He was a ray of light in the darkness of RCMP bureaucracy. Someone inside cared.

The issue with medical forms and computer access were technical obstacles that I knew were placed in my path by D Division to aggravate me. It worked. The many small problems would occasionally become overwhelming and I would have to deal with each one as it came up. I had been reinstated as an officer as of December 2, 1999, and all benefits and pay cheques were to have been forwarded to me and adjusted on the RCMP computer. This did not happen. For several weeks I did not receive any money and despite making phone calls to Pay Section at D Division, I was given the same song and dance: "We are working on it", "It is a new system", "Sorry, your severance pay was accidentally sent to you and you have to send it back."

I waited for the paperwork to arrive indicating my police identification number had been entered onto the RCMP system and I was again covered by insurance. Also, I wanted confirmation the documents relating to my grievances had been received. There continued to be barriers and complications on the grievances and the complaint against Sergeant Medder. All letters, correspondence and responses copied and filed at my home and with my lawyer.

In an attempt to make my situation for employment more marketable, I continued to pursue my education at my own expense by attending Red River College, taking courses in Human Resources and Computer Training. With additional qualifications, I hoped my chances of finding a non–operational position within the RCMP would be increased.

The long wait between the different decisions on the grievances was discouraging. At this time there were over thirty different stages in the grievance process from start to finish. The two levels of decisions were made by senior RCMP officers, the grievance would then be sent to the External Review Committee (consisting of three lawyers independent of the RCMP) and these recommendations were given to the Commissioner who made the final decision on the Level 11.

Looking back at all my notes and documentation, I really found it hard to believe I had stuck it out so long, wishing of returning to work, and having a successful career in the RCMP. My lawyer kept telling me the RCMP were in violation of the Canadian Labour Laws in their failure to "accommodate" a person with disabilities. The Supreme Court of Canada has stated that employers should be 'innovative yet practical in seeking "accommodation." It was hope.

I just had to press on and not give up. Gaining new information about policies and internal news from the RCMP was difficult. Any information regarding procedure changes and pay updates I received from John. He worked at another detachment but provided a good support system for me with regard to the mentality of the RCMP and decision processes. No one from D Division forwarded important news or made any effort to inform me about policy or any changes which would have an effect on my grievances.

It seemed at every turn, deliberately thwarted by officers of the RCMP. I tried not to take it personally but I truly felt like an outcast. from the RCMP "family." More than once I would ask myself, "Why do I keep this up? Why don't I just quit?" Perhaps I needed to find the answer.

In June, my lawyer, Roger Bond, again sent a powerful letter to the Human Resources Officer in Ottawa who was handling my grievance. In this letter he again requested information regarding other disabled officers who had been "accommodated" by the RCMP and the nature of their disabilities. He included several case studies to back up his request for this information. The RCMP's outdated policies clearly violated the Supreme Court of Canada ruling in the duty to "accommodate" in the work place, an issue the RCMP obviously ignored. My lawyer also requested changes in the wording of the Medical Discharge document. His letter states, "Cst. Benson has not been treated equitably in that since her grievance she has been denied access to the local RCMP detachment in her area of Gimli." He asked why my badge had not been returned. Why was

I not allowed to write the Corporal exam? Why is the inequality continuing? These grievances were to forwarded to the External Review Board prior to being submitted to the Commissioner. It was great to get a copy of that letter while checking my emails. It was a good left hook to the chin of the RCMP.

Another Nail
In The Coffin Of The RCMP

IT SEEMED EVERY DAY WHEN I WENT TO THE MAIL I received some sort of bad news or a letter demanding an immediate response. I did just that, I sent in responses and requested time extensions when my lawyer needed more time. I did everything by the RCMP's own policies.

In the summer of 2000, David had gone to Quebec for seven weeks of training with the military. He had decided to go into an area of service for career advancement. It was difficult to be newly married and getting used to that arrangement with my daughter. I felt the stress of the grievances, and with my husband away in Quebec City for several weeks, I was lonely. However, I managed to keep things afloat at home by spending time with my daughter, doing the yard work and trying to keep ahead of the smothering amount of paper work and deadlines involved with the grievances. File folder after folder filled with documents.

In mid July 2000, I received the decision from the Commanding Officer Featherstone, of D Division, on the Level 1 Grievance, Medical Discharge. He denied us access to medical information on other injured officers and the accommodations arranged with them, on the basis it violated their privacy. He reiterated that a proper Force-wide job search had been done in seeking a suitable position to fit my medical profile. Although I found this upsetting, and promptly forwarded the Level II part of the grievance, which meant the entire grievance sent to a more senior officer in Ottawa and eventually the Commissioner. Another long wait was just beginning.

My medical profile continued to be left out of the computer from December 1999 to August 2000. Again I called the Pay Section, and again asked the reason for the delay. According to Pay Section, the delay in updating my medical number onto the computer was resting in Sergeant Fauxl's office. Why was I not surprised? In my opinion, he was not at all interested in my welfare. The RCMP had never had to deal with a feisty Icelander who is not loud but tries again and again. A solution seemed so obvious: just find a position requiring the use of my skills and education. I knew of various job positions within the RCMP which did not require carrying a gun.

As this grievance process dragged on year after year, I became more convinced no one wanted, or was willing, to take responsibility for doing something proactive. Individual officers who stand up to the organization are targeted as "trouble makers" which results in further isolation and harassment. I continued to call Pay Section, questioning delays in receiving cheques and benefits. I would call the Health Service Office regarding my medical number. I called Staffing and Personnel regarding time extensions, delays and the status of my grievances. Wherever I turned for answers or direction, there were none. I would be told, "The RCMP has never done that," or "this is how we always do it." Their inability to think outside the box caused my grievances to last almost ten years. What a waste of resources. In my mind, there was no logical reason for such a misuse of time except to wear me down with psychological harassment.

September came along with more denials for my Income Tax Adjustment grievance. This issue was separate from the Medical Discharge grievance and I had to ensure I followed the timelines request for extension where necessary. All grievances follow the same process and proceed from Level l to Level II. Each decision can be grieved. The issue for the Income Tax Adjustment grievance was the refusal to acknowledge my stress leave was duty related and the refusal to indicate the correct days

Inspector Embrouille refused to acknowledge the connection between my stress-related illness and duty-related injury. The two are entwined and would not miraculously heal overnight. Therefore, if I was off sick for the months between August 21, 1998 and December 31, 1998, how would I suddenly be fit for duty the next day in January? The Inspector flatly refused to follow Workers' Compensation guidelines. Several weeks later, in November, an officer from the Gimli Detachment came to my home and handed me a folded piece of paper, a fax copy of the names on the Grievance Advisory Board (GAB). Her comment was, "Sergeant Medder told me to give this to you." It was not in an envelope for privacy, just folded. The document required me to sign saying I accepted the names on the (GAB). The function of this Board is to examine all documents submitted by the parties involved in the grievance and to ensure all policies and Force regulations are being adhered to. I waited a few more weeks for the report.

When it arrived, the decision was no surprise to me. The three-person board unanimously recommended the grievance against the Medical Board be denied. Therefore, I had to continue to the next level. I faxed off a copy to my lawyer. Another Christmas had come and gone again with no resolution in sight. I kept plugging along day after day, week after week and now year after year.

Although I had high hopes for 2001, it began on a sad note. David and I were trying to have a baby. I managed to get pregnant but it did not last long as a result of a minor fender bender. While driving to my class one winter night in January, a car pulled into my lane of traffic and I hit the one in front of me, my first car accident. During class felt ill and had to get a friend to drive me home. On the way home we stopped at the hospital to get me checked out as my head was pounding and I felt ill. Sadly, while on holiday a month later I miscarried. Three weeks after the accident, David, Nadine and I flew to London, England. Nadine was to stay for nine days, then fly home. It was spectacular to see all the tourist places that are on postcards: the Tower of London, Big Ben, St. Paul's Cathedral, Westminster Abbey, Buckingham Palace, and to ride the red double-decker buses. It was expensive to holiday in England, so we took the train or bus to most places, or walked. Being a police officer, I wanted to see Scotland Yard. However, the security was strict and without my RCMP identification, I was not allowed in the secure part of the building. The Recruiting Officer was interested in recruiting David and me to join their police force. We left the office with a bottle opener and two applications to complete back in Canada. Apparently there is a need for constables in London. David and I planned to travel the countryside for another five days for a delayed honeymoon. Regrettably, we never did make it. One morning, I had terrible pain and a doctor was called to our hotel. Upon an examination it was determined I was pregnant and should fly home immediately. Unfortunately, I lost the baby shortly after our return to Canada, which only added to my misery.

A decision from the (GAB) was officially served on me January 23, 2001, denying my grievance for Income Tax Adjustment. This Board gives recommendations prior to forwarding a Level 1 Grievance. (GAB) letter recommended 'that the griever did not have standing and the grievance can be set aside accordingly. Alternatively, it was determined "that the griever does have standing, the GAB recommends that the grievance be denied in respect of January 1, 1998 to August 20, 1998 as the griever was fit for alternative duties during this period. The tax certification for the period of August 20, 1998 and December 3 1998 should be maintained and furthered to read August 21, 1998 to December 31, 1998 as this was interpreted as a typographical error by Dr. Jupe."

There was actually no confusion as to the dates. This was another way of trying to correct a mix up. There had been many documents and letters back and forth between Dr. Jupe's office, Inspector Embrouille, and myself where this 'mistake in dates' would have been noticed. I did not agree with the reasoning and with the timeline for a response approaching, my lawyer had sent off our response to the GAB's report, including a request this grievance be forwarded to the External Review Committee (ERC). This Committee is made up of lawyers who know the law, Canadian Human Rights and the RCMP's own policies, and would therefore be objective in their decisions. I hoped once an intelligent person would read my grievance, the discrimination and inequality would become obvious. Time would prove this to be an accurate assessment.

I could not imagine the RCMP bungling could not get any worse. I was wrong. While reading a copy of our RCMP Gazette, I noticed my name was in there as 'a re-engaged officer' and with an incorrect date. I was furious and immediately sent a letter to Sgt. Fauxl addressing my concerns. He did not respond to this letter nor to the second letter sent to him a month later. In May he finally sent a response concerning the return of my badge, the status of benefits and the erroneous report of my re-engagement dated September 2000. It was errors of this nature that made me extremely angry and frustrated with the whole process. My main concern was this would affect any pension for the future as broken service can reduce the amount of a pension.

At the end of March I received a copy of the decision from the GAB, denying my grievance against the Medical Discharge. The decision was based on a previous case of an injured officer hurt on the job. I found there were copies of many documents missing in the report directly related to the specifics of my case. I realized I needed to have more time to review the report in detail. I received a copy of my entire case that was to be forwarded to the External Review Committee in Ottawa, and I had to go through the entire file looking for any detail which might have been left out. As there were over 200 pages, requested a time extension in order to be thorough. Roger and I found many errors which needed to be corrected or required further clarification and, in my opinion, the report failed to show the abuse of power D Division had inflicted during the grievance process: the phone calls, numerous letters, uncooperative senior staff and the refusal to allow me to write the Corporal's exam.

In June 2001 we forwarded the changes and additional documentation necessary for a complete and honest evaluation of the events of the Medical Discharge proceedings. By August the additional papers for the grievance were ready to be added to the report sent to the External Review Committee in Ottawa. Then all we had to do was wait some more for the light to come on in someone's head. The summer months were typical, my daughter finished school and David went to Quebec City to complete his training with the military. I was stressed out worrying about how this saga with the RCMP would unfold. Deep inside, I knew time was running out but did not know the end was just around the corner.

The End Is In Sight,
Do I Trust The RCMP?

IN OCTOBER, I RECEIVED A CALL TO GO TO THE GIMLI detachment for service of documents. I went to the detachment on November 5, 2001 to get a copy of the decision on the Medical Discharge grievance Level 11. The decision was to be forwarded to the External Review Committee as per my request. Despite my fear of losing my job, I did some exciting news.

Finally, after so many months of hoping, I found out that same day I was pregnant. I was so excited, and David and Nadine were just as excited as I was. My doctor put me on bed rest as I had miscarried in January and there was some danger of losing this baby. I took his words to heart and for over a week remained at home, with no exercising or lifting. I had some cramps one day and started to bleed. In a panic I called the hospital and was told to come in the next day. I tried to remain calm but I knew it was too late. The next day I went to the hospital in Gimli and was admitted for the next few days. I lost the baby that night. I cried and cried. One nurse came in to administer a drip to increase the contractions to 'remove what was still inside'. I started to sob so hard that I could not breathe. This nurse offered no words of comfort, which only added to my despair.

Fortunately, my body recovered and I was reassured that I could still get pregnant. Optimistically, I believed in this dream. David had a hard time watching me suffer over our loss. Nadine had a difficult time seeing her strong mommy devastated at loosing the baby. I let myself feel all the pain and as Christmas approached prepared two decorations for the tree, one for each baby I lost that year. I had names for them both, Isabella (my grandmother's name) and James (I like that name). I had spoken with my therapist several times during the few weeks after my miscarriage to deal with the loss. I also needed to find a way to let go and my making the decorations ensured they would not be forgotten. I found a sense of peace and acceptance of the losses. Christmas was emotionally difficult for me, being with my family and other happy people who did not know how to talk to or support me. They simply could not understand why at our age, David and I wanted a baby, and as a result could not comprehend our feelings. I think the grief was two-fold: first, the loss of my pregnancies and the hopes and dreams that come with having children; the other was the loss of my job and hopes of a promising career. As the end of 2001 approached, I began to wonder if this battle would ever end. It was not until February 14, 2002, that I got my answer.

My lawyer, Roger, called that day and asked if I was sitting down. I could sense the excitement in his voice as he began to read the decision from the External Review Board on my grievance against the Medical Discharge. He said, "Sherry, I have great news. I have just received a copy of the decision from the External Review Board, and their findings support all your issues. They agreed you should be accommodated, that the RCMP failed in treating you fairly in regards to looking for a position and the RCMP should have offered you training." And he laughed.

I started to scream and scream. David, my long supportive husband, came running to see what happened. I was crying I was so happy. Finally, after all this time, vindication! Roger added this was the recommendation from the External Review Board and this decision has been forwarded to the Commissioner who will make the final decision. The External Review Board is made up of three independent lawyers who examine the grievance, all documents, and render their recommendations to the Commissioner who follows these suggestions. The Commissioner, who is not a lawyer, does not change a decision recommended by the Board. This was so fantastic! I just had to wait a few more months for the Commissioner to render his decision. I screamed again and jumped up and down yelling, "Who is the man, I'm da man!" over and over again. That rush of adrenaline and what a relief! After such a long time in this grievance process, I could not believe it was almost over. The stress and strain for all these years was almost over. The financial concern of loosing my job was coming to an end. I thought of the many times I had cried out of the frustration and pain at being harassed by the RCMP, the arguments with family and friends in defending my decision and the continued struggle. The many times I doubted the course of action I was taking, the sleepless nights, the anxiety in getting the mail or answering the phone for fear of more bad news from the RCMP. This was almost over!

David, Nadine and I went out for dinner to celebrate the long-awaited good news. I called my sister and parents to let them know. My father was happy: "Way to go, Lambie." (Lambie was my nickname from childhood because of my fuzzy blond hair.) My mother said, "Congratulations." All their reactions were positive. However, the real relief was knowing that this fight was over and my hopes for a satisfying career were still alive.

I had to wait for the Commissioner's official decision and that would take a few more months. I continued taking courses at Red River College in Winnipeg, in order to complete my second diploma. I felt with this extra training, my opportunities would be greater for employment in various sections of the RCMP. It was easy waiting a few more months for the official decision, as I knew the judgment would be in my favor. It was complete vindication.

On August 28, 2002, I was officially served the decision from the Commissioner. An officer from Selkirk detachment called to say that he had a document that needed to be hand-served and asked if he could drive out to my house. I agreed. As he approached my drive way, I met him outside. I still had that protective feeling regarding any RCMP coming into my house. I could not help but have a big smile on my face because I knew what to expect in this decision. There was an awkward tension between myself and the officer nevertheless I held my ground, and when asked, did not reveal any details as to the content of the document. He drove away and I ran into the house to read it in private. I was so excited.

Roger was correct in his prediction, the Commissioner did, in fact, make the same recommendations as the External Review Board in February. The Commissioner confirmed that a complete overhaul of the grievance process was necessary. "Accommodation" for dis-abled officers was to be enacted and duties must be re-bundled to fit the medical profile of the officer whose knowledge, skills and interests were to be taken into account in this process, to allow the officer to maintain dignity in the workplace and to have equal career oppor-tunities. Also, the report found that D Division had failed making in the Force-wide search and had failed to recognize my knowledge and education in determining a position for me within the RCMP. The words jumped out at me like flashing neon signs. So exciting! I had copies of the faxes that had been sent from D Division to the other divisions across Canada. The request for placement came from the Officer in Charge of Staffing in Ottawa, the RCMP Headquarters. The Commissioner's decision on my grievance was vindication for my claims.

It was a complete victory, yet I was apprehensive about returning to work for the RCMP. I did not trust the process and feared I could be subjected to some form of retribution from the very officers who had been so cruel and deceptive all through the years. Many of the officers who had had the opportunity to assist me in the grievance process, and did not do so, were still working in the very building where I would to be working. The Commissioner's decision made it quite clear that D Division had failed in many areas. Therefore, I am sure some of these same officers had gotten their hands slapped. It has been my experience officers in a position of power have a long memory when they are annoyed.

Within a few days I received a call from Staffing at D Division, requesting an appointment to discuss my return to work. The Staffing Section of the RCMP is similar to Human Resources. I was nervous about meeting someone from Staffing as my experience with persons from that section had not been good up to this point. The next day I received another call, from Stanley Smith of Employee Services, working at D Division, advising me that the meeting would be with him instead of an RCMP officer from Staffing. We scheduled an appointment at Earl's Restaurant at Polo Park in Winnipeg and met a few days later to discuss what I needed to return to work, and what type of position I could see myself enjoying.

I met with Stanley and we discussed my six-year grievance, the turmoil I had endured and the harassment by members of the very organization in which I was trying so desperately to maintain my position. I explained the pain and suffering I had tolerated and the feelings of isolation from the RCMP. He said he was acting on behalf of the Assistant Commissioner of D Division Thomas Smith (no relation to Stanley). Some of the issues I said I wanted resolved were the return of my badge and payment for the education I had taken during the last six years. I suggested many different positions I would be capable of performing within the RCMP which were non-operational, such as Human Resources, Recruitment and Selection, Alternative

Dispute Resolution. The RCMP Human Resources had various sections where I would be able to physically perform, and with my new training, was now qualified for. The Alternative Dispute Resolution program helps officers resolve problems without the formal process of a grievance. This section was not in existence six years ago. In retrospect, perhaps someone in D Division could have saved six years of my life. I brought up the idea of an RCMP Wellness Officer, a person who keeps in contact with the officers who are on extended sick leave, officers dealing with medical boards, stress leave and the discharge process to keep them in the loop as to their rights and policies. This would ensure the officer would not feel isolated and forgotten. I know it would have helped me. I also agreed to take further training in these areas.

It was important to voice how the RCMP had completely abandoned me during my grievance. I was not allowed into the local detachment and was harassed by various officers through no fault of my own. There was no one in the organization from whom I could get information, requests for forms or policies, except John French. At that time the Division Representatives were ineffective and less-than-willing to help someone who, from their perspective, was causing trouble. I wanted to help anyone else avoid the same experience. I also addressed my concern about what plans the RCMP at D Division had for me. Could I trust them? To date my dealings with D Division had been a constant struggle. I had sent copies of my completed courses to Sergeant Fauxl to have them added to my education file which would help in finding me a job, but he returned them saying any education would be added if I was successful with the grievance. I wanted this addressed. I expected a position which would utilize my skills and education and not be demeaning in nature.

Another issue we addressed was the percentage of disability for my duty-related shoulder injury, and Income Tax Adjustment for 1999 to 2002. My outstanding grievance for the amended T–4 had been going on for the last three years. I asked what could be done to resolve that. Stanley assured me having the authority from the Assistant Commissioner of D Division, the required documents would be forthcoming.

My gut feeling was telling me to first get the money for legal and school fees, the tax adjustment and a confirmation of a position to best fit my knowledge, skills and interest, prior to returning to work. However, I thought I would trust D Division. I had hoped the experience of pursuing my rights for six years had taught them a lesson, to treat officers with dignity and equality. How wrong I was.

Several days later, September 7, 2002, I sent a letter, confirming my requests and stating I also had a record of what was discussed regarding positions of employment. I waited to see what would happen. What job was I going to do? How would I feel about working for the organization that tried so hard to get rid of me? These questions were on my mind night and day as I waited for the letter from D Division.

After several weeks, I called Stanley Smith to ask if a letter was coming soon with regard to the job. He indicated he would send it to me shortly. I waited another week or two. During this time I went to a Military dinner with David. General Ray Henault was the speaker. As the General was thanking out-of-town guests, he noted the RCMP Assistant Commissioner Thomas Smith was also attending. I scanned the audience to see who this person was and what he looked like. I wanted to see the man who had power over my career. I recognized him as he tipped his head in acknowledgement. He was a tall man, with graying brown hair, a long nose and pale skin. He had the smile of a politician, whose lips are smiling but whose eyes are not. Once the General had finished his speech and the audience was getting ready to leave, I approached the Assistant Commissioner and introduced myself. He looked surprised for a second and quickly regained his composure. I asked about when the letter was coming regarding a position at D Division. He said "You should receive a letter within the next few days, and I know that you will be pleased with what we have for you". I thanked him and left for home with a renewed sense of hope of having a great career with the RCMP. All the way home I was excited in the hopes of a good job. Again was I wrong.

One morning when returning home from Gimli, after having driven my daughter to school, I noticed a northbound police car turn and follow me. As the vehicle approached, I recognized the driver as a Sergeant from Selkirk detachment. I had a feeling he had something to serve on me, so I waited for him to activate the police lights, however the lights did not go on. I thought maybe I was being paranoid. I decided to get my mail in Winnipeg Beach and also to determine if, in fact, the police car was following me. As I was about to get out of my car at the Post Office, the police vehicle pulled up beside me and the driver rolled down his window, handed me an envelope and said, "I didn't want to pull you over. I went to your house and you were not home and then went to your sister-in-law's to see where you could be. She said you may be in Gimli so I headed for Gimli when I spotted you." I took the letter, all the while thinking, "I am getting a bad feeling about this." The letter he gave me was from D Division. Once he was gone I opened it, read it and felt as though I had just been kicked in the stomach – that nauseating feeling of doom.

There were two letters, one from a Staffing Officer at D Division, and a letter from the supervisor of Commercial Crime Section advising me of my new position and the duties I would be doing in this section. I was crushed. The letter from Staffing told me I must attend Commercial Crime Section at D Division within fourteen days of receipt of this letter. I was trapped, forced to go to a job I had never asked for, nor did I have any qualifications for this section. Not only that, the duties outlined in the letter looked like secretarial responsibilities. Back at home, I called Stanley Smith of Employee Services to ask what had happened; this section was not mentioned at our meeting. He indicated that "There are Human Resource jobs within

D Division but they are funded out of North West Region in Regina and the Deputy Commissioner told Assistant Commissioner Thomas Smith to find a job for you."

I said, "This is not an offer but an order. Did you know about this, Stanley, when we met and discussed the various areas in which I would be able to perform within the RCMP? I never considered this section and this letter is way out in left field." I was angry and frustrated. He had no response and I ended the conversation. Needless to say the next few minutes in my kitchen were clouded with a string of considerably less than ladylike words. I regained my composure and set out a plan of what I needed to do right know to try to fix this mess. My 'gut' feeling was telling me "I told you this would happen!"

I faxed copies of the letters to my lawyer, Roger Bond in Winnipeg. Roger sent a letter on November 4th, 2002 to Sgt. Glenna of Staffing, indicating that he continued to act as my solicitor and questioned the reasoning of sending me to Commercial Crime when I was not qualified, nor had I asked for this section. In his letter, Roger also addressed the issue of Sergeant Fauxl returning the transcript of my marks, in February, which clearly showed my area of education, and suggested with the number of RCMP officers across Canada, surely a position in Human Resources could be found. I was not asking for the "perfect job," I was asking to be "accommodated" in an area where I would use my knowledge, skills, interest and abilities, while maintaining dignity in the workplace and career advancement. A copy was also faxed to new Commissioner of the RCMP. I wondered what the new Commissioner was thinking, being bombarded by letters and faxes, all with my name on them.

Several days later I received a call from Selkirk Detachment to come to Selkirk to get a letter. I drove to Selkirk, knowing the letter was in response to my lawyer's letter of November 4th. I was right, the letter came from the Assistant Commissioner Thomas Smith. In this letter he ordered me to be at Commercial Crime Section at D

Division in Winnipeg on November 20, 2002 and that failure to do so would result in being charged under the RCMP Act and Regulations. I felt I had no choice, and was again being held hostage in a job with no future. Again I was right.

With this feeling of doom and failure, I cried for hours. I kept re-reading the letter in utter shock. "How could this happen? After all I went through? I was still being mentally beaten! What are my options? Do I want to quit? Then what? I have no money to live!"

All the changes in policies which were a direct result of the success of my six year grievance were not benefiting me in any way. It was demoralizing. David tried to cheer me up and encouraged me to try Commercial Crime. He got me to realize that I am a strong person and not a failure, and perhaps some good can come out of this. I began to prepare myself for Commercial Crime and to look toward the future with the possibility of moving to another section after a few months. I decided to do my best at making this 'accommodation' work. I went to my lawyer's office to discuss my options with him. I asked for advice on this situation and what to do as if I were his sister or wife. He did not hesitate, just said, "Grieve and obey." This meant I would be at Commercial Crime Section the next morning and would continue with the grievance if the accommodation was not working. Roger then sent a letter out to Assistant Commissioner Smith advising him of my intention to make this 'accommodation' work but advising him also I am not giving up any of my legal rights should this process fail. In some ways I still had hope but it was clouded with doubt. There was tightness in my chest, I felt like a drowning person not able to hold onto a life preserver.

Later that night I called my therapist for a two-hour session dealing with my hopes and fears of returning to work for an organization which had clearly shown inequality and intimidation of dissenters would continue. My therapist helped me deal with the fears of being "set up" by the RCMP and going to a job about which I knew nothing.

I could hardly sleep all night and awoke before the alarm at 6:30 am. David and I drove mostly in silence. He held my hand and every few minutes would say, "You will be okay, just give it a couple of weeks." My mind was racing with questions, and anxiety about the unknown. How would David know what this was like? He was never in a position like this. I was the main player. My first reaction to his comments was anger. Slowly I recognized he was trying to be supportive. As we drove up to the building I felt my heart flutter and stomach turn over. All of a sudden the fear of going into the lion's den was almost overwhelming, making me sweat and want to turn around for the safety of home. Pushing through the terror and fear gripping my chest, I looked up at the four-storey grey building, thinking 'I am here, after six years, all the pain and suffering; I am still here with the RCMP. I have to stay alert and be strong.' I got out of the car, slowly, as if walking the last few steps to an execution, turned to look at David, as if to gather some strength from him. He had a smile on his face but I could tell he was concerned about me. I smiled back, took in a deep breath and walked through the doors. I thought, 'Here goes'. I had no idea where these few steps would take me.

My Best Foot Forward

STAFF/SERGEANT ALLAN MACDOUGAL WAS A TALL MAN with blue eyes, glasses, graying hair, and a pleasant smile. He made me feel welcome as soon as he shook my hand. I could tell almost immediately he had a good sense of humour, because he made a joke about the size of my teeth. "I can see you need a super size tube of toothpaste."

I laughed. "They don't call me Constable Colgate for nothing." He laughed.

We rode the elevator up to the third floor and he introduced me to everyone in our section and asked that they join us for coffee in a few minutes. I was shown to the office which I would be sharing with another officer, Corporal Pierre Joyau. Pierre is from Quebec and has a loud, friendly laugh. Over the next few months I learned to really appreciate his hard work and sense of humour. I felt all the officers working on Commercial Crime wanted to be in this section and appeared to be content.

After having coffee in the cafeteria, I was taken to the identification room to get a building pass. Allan took me around the four story building, built in the 1970's style with an atrium in the middle and offices around the outside. The only offices with which I was familiar were Staffing and the cafeteria, so I was pleased to be familiarized with the various sections, the location of the mail room, washrooms and gym area. Later during that day Allan came back to see how I was doing and said, "I have something for you, it has been in Sergeant Fauxl's office. Here." With that he dropped my badge on my desk. I looked up at him and smiled, "I have been waiting a long time for this to happen, thank you very, very much." He said, "You did the work." After he left I stared at my RCMP badge for a long time. I began to think differently about being here. Perhaps it would be tolerable for a few months; I decided to give this my best shot. I knew being a hard worker would pay off for me in the end.

Stanley Smith showed up later in the afternoon to see how I was doing. We walked to the elevators for some privacy and stood by the balcony. I was angry at his deception in not telling me the Human Resource positions are filled by an Officer in Regina, Saskatchewanian and not D Division. He made a feeble attempt to make it look like he knew nothing about me going to Commercial Crime. He suggested, "If you are not happy here, if things don't work out, don't feel you are stuck, there could be options." I asked about the issue of repayment of the school and legal fees as agreed upon at our meeting in September 2002. He said the Assistant Commissioner was working hard to make this accommodation work.

I said, "So am I, and the only thing that makes me angry is when people promise one thing and do another. The fact that you said there were Constable positions in H.R., then sent a letter to my lawyer saying there were none, for example."

Stanley said, "I meant that there are positions but none which are currently available." I asked why the discrepancy in the Constable positions and why could he not have told me earlier. He could offer no answer but backpedaled in his response: "There are term positions but these are finished in December and we did not think that would be good for you." Again he reassured me that Assistant Commissioner Smith wanted to assist in this situation and I should let him know if I was not happy in Commercial Crime.

As he spoke his cell phone, which was attached to his belt, it flew off and fell three floors down. I wondered if the spirits of former RCMP officers were present. We both looked over the balcony and watched it break on the floor of the atrium.

I flatly stated, "Good thing no one was hit by that." Inside I was giggling as I returned to my office.

Over the next few weeks I found myself very tired. My shoulder injury, the disability over which the whole grievance process started in 1996, bothered me at night as it had been doing for years. The ache and pain in the shoulder caused me to move many times during the night and as a result, I had disturbed sleep, flipping from side to side. Before I started work I was used to not having a restful sleep, however, having to get up and drive for an hour made it even more difficult to get the necessary rest. By Friday night I was so tired all I could do was eat and sleep. Rarely could I attend social functions either RCMP or non-RCMP on Fridays because I was exhausted. It had been like that for years and affected my alertness.

I continued trying to make this work. I showed up every day willing to learn and assist in any duty assigned, knowing or believing this was only temporary. I felt excited to work and was full of hope for my future. As December approached, I planned to take holidays. I had accumulated many days of holiday over the six years of the grievance.

I was asked to go to the office of Sergeant Harold Front on December 24th, 2002 which was the day of our staff Christmas party to discuss my "accommodation." Sergeant Harold Front from Staffing and Personnel wanted to see me and determine how I was doing and what my plans were for the next five years. I told him that although the staff on Commercial Crime had made me feel welcome, it was obvious my absence from the RCMP organization had affected any investigative experience needed to perform in this highly specialized section. My supervisor, Staff/Sergeant Allan MacDougal agreed with me this is not a good fit. My plans for the next five years were to be promoted, finish my degree in Conflict Resolution and Mediation, and to work in Alternative Dispute Resolution Section, or a similar field. Sergeant Front told me that I "must prove myself to the RCMP that I want to be here and that there is no bitterness."

I said, "I am willing to do my very best to make this 'accommodation' work but I am not trained for Commercial Crime and not able to be promoted."

He agreed it would only be for six months and at that time I would be moved to a more appropriate section to fit my skills. I was happy with that. Once again I was looking forward to having a successful career in an area where my knowledge and skills would be utilized. I returned to the Christmas party.

In early January 2003, I went to the Commercial Crime Course in Regina for two weeks. I enjoyed learning different areas within this section, meeting officers from other provinces and I entertained the hope of having a new chance at improving my career. At that time I thought perhaps I would be promoted and work in this section. However, as the course continued, I realized there was so much I was not able to do as an investigator, due to my injury, and would not be able to leave the office. This was discouraging. As I was not able to carry a gun or drive a police car due to my disability, the only duties left for me were clerical and to act as an assistant to other investigators. I felt I was right back where I started six years ago in Selkirk being assigned as an assistant to the detachment support staff. All this was very disappointing, knowing in this section my only career would be that of a glorified secretary. I began to look forward to the end of the six months. Upon my return from the course in Regina, I spoke with my supervisor, Staff/Sergeant Allan MacDougal, expressing my concern over my situation. He agreed there was no opportunity for me to be promoted in this section due to my lack of experience and education in the Commercial Crime field, and my inability to leave the office to gain experience in search warrants and interviews of witnesses.

Staff/Sergeant Allan MacDougal asked how long I was going to be injured. I was shocked and had no idea he knew nothing of my injury. I could not understand why my supervisor had deliberately not been told my disability was permanent. The officers in Staffing had not revealed the extent of my injury. He had thought I would physically improve to the condition required of an operational officer. I had to tell him the whole story, about my disability, the six-year grievance and the reason for being ordered to work in Commercial Crime. I offered to give him a copy of the Commissioner's decision if he needed more details.

Allan sat there and listened, and then he leaned forward and said, "Sherry, I read the Commissioner's decision on your grievance, and I was wondering whose cornflakes did you piss in to have such trouble?"

Smiling I said, "I simply would not let them medically discharge me for my duty-related injury when the RCMP had been accommodating men for years." He agreed the RCMP was not fair and he would do his best to help me get into a position best suited to my abilities and interest. Allan was a man who was blunt and straight to the point. I liked his style and honesty. I trusted him and he trusted me.

I worked for the next six months to prove I was a good worker, had a strong work ethic and was willing to show I was an asset to the RCMP team in the hopes of being moved to a more appropriate position. Staff/Sergeant MacDougal told to me on several occasions he had spoken to Staffing and Inspector Victor Belling, in charge of Economic Crime Section, but they refused to move me. I could tell he felt sorry for me and that he was helpless to improve the situation. My duties included filing, listening to statements, which were taped and typed, making the necessary corrections, photocopying thousands and thousands of documents. It felt like being a hostage, kept against my will with no one willing to help. I came to work everyday with a smile, refused to let anyone see I was unhappy. Remember it was only for six months.

I remained in contact with Stanley Smith of Employee Services, via email and phone calls. The following officers also received similar emails and phone calls on my accommodation; Chief Superintendent Tim Skavinski of Professional Standards and External Review Directorate, Craig Noman D Division Representative, Assistant Commissioner Thomas Smith D Division, Superintendent Jerry Kayen Human Resource Officer Northwest Region, Regina. However, according to Stanley the officers in Staffing did not listen to them either. These emails were all comparable in nature: "Have you any news as to the payment of the school and legal fees? Has anyone made a decision on the above noted?" or "This borderlines on ridiculous." One email to Superintendent Gerry Kayen was a little more forward: "I would like an answer as to the date when I shall be receiving the above noted. I believe that my having to wait for over a year is completely unreasonable. Thank you." These went back and forth to Stanley Smith, Sergeant Fauxl, Sergeant Noman and Superintendent Gerry Kayen for months, all to no avail. Confusing?

My lawyer, Roger Bond, sent a follow up letter to the Commissioner explaining to him the situation I was in and why, in his opinion, this was not an 'accommodation'. In April of 2003, Staff/Sergeant Allan MacDougal retired after over 30 years of service. I was sorry to see him go. He was an honest man whom I had come to consider an ally. We frequently had coffee to discuss the unsatisfactory solution the RCMP of D Division had reached with regard to my situation.

In June 2003, I met with Sergeant Harold Front who informed me I needed another six months to prove myself.

I told him, "I am not happy in Commercial Crime. I find the work embarrassing and not satisfying in any way. I am unable to be promoted and am getting farther behind other officers who did not have to go through a six year absence."

He did not seem to be concerned about my difficulties with the accommodation in Commercial Crime. "Well, Sherry, you appear to be enjoying the work on Commercial Crime. According to your assessment the supervisors are pleased with your effort."

I responded, "Just because I don't walk around with 'gloom and doom' on my face doesn't mean I am happy working in Commercial Crime. I have no interest at all in this section. My skills are not in this area."

I left interview feeling very discouraged. As I walked back to my office I thought, "Well, maybe six more months is not that long, but I am going to continue to educate myself in the areas in which I'm interested." I figured once I had a degree or diploma in Conflict Resolution, Mediation or another related field, the RCMP would make an effort to improve the 'accommodation'. I was very wrong.

From the time of my return to work in November, I continued to wait for the payment of the school and legal fees. This was now six months. I spoke with our Division Representative, Sergeant Craig Noman, who sent emails to various offices trying to determine who would make a decision and when payment would be made. We got the run-around for over sixteen months, from Sergeant Fauxl and Sergeant Lucas, on the payment of the fees. Finally I had had enough and sent a brief email in April 2004 to the Commissioner in Ottawa, asking why there was such a delay in D Division on the return of fees which had been agreed upon in September of 2002. This caused the situation to move a bit.

Again, in November 2003, I made the march up to the fourth floor staffing office to speak with Sergeant Front to request a move to a more suitable position. I went in and politely told him why I wanted to be moved: "Being an assistant for almost a year is fine but not what I want for the next nine years. I want job satisfaction and career advancement, neither of which I am getting as a glorified secretary. What is next for me?"

Sergeant Front listened and calmly said "Well Sherry, we have decided to keep you in Commercial Crime for another two years. We think that is what is best for you."

Stunned, I asked, "What did Assistant Commissioner Smith say about the section to which I should go? What did he tell you about my situation?"

Sergeant Front replied "He told me to 'make good by her', and so we sent you to Commercial Crime".

I was furious and, tossing caution to the wind, the tone in my voice going deeper, I said, "Well, being in Commercial Crime is not good by me! I will not stay in this section for another two years. There is no way!" I got up and left, determined to go over this man's head. Once again, I was in a position where I had to fight for my rights. The agreement upon my return in November 2002 was I should be on Commercial Crime for a "little while." This turned into six months for me to prove myself, and after working hard for that period, another six months added. Now I was told my stay in Commercial Crime would be another two years. That would make me nine years behind other officers and no further ahead in my career than before I returned to work.

The thought of doing this demeaning job for two more years almost drove me over the edge of sanity. I felt my situation was hopeless and the very situation I had feared was developing right before my eyes. The RCMP was paying me back for standing up for equality and fair treatment. Now I wanted to make the RCMP pay for all the years of suffering. It was a terrible few days.

I phoned my therapist as I was concerned about falling apart. I felt so betrayed, alone and humiliated at doing the job I was forced to do. The session was dominated by my feeling of betrayal, not only by the RCMP in D Division but within myself. I had to admit that my instinct told me to bargain first before returning to work back in November 2002. Memories of Tisdale were ever present in my mind. I had wanted to be nice and this is where my niceness put me. My therapist helped me see there were options available and to utilize the access I had within the RCMP. I needed a plan to stay sane at work, to figure out what to do at work every day to keep from falling apart or breaking down completely. Together with my therapist, I decided that walking to Tim Horton's every day would be one way of keeping my sanity. For the remainder of my time working at Commercial Crime, that is exactly what I did every day, usually alone, to get a Tim Horton's coffee. It was a quiet way of taking control of my life. After our conversation, I felt exhausted. My eyes were swollen and red from crying and releasing the anger deep inside me. On the flip-side, complete mental exhaustion helped me sleep.

At the end of the week, I had a meeting with my supervisors with regard to my yearly assessment. During the year on Commercial Crime, I assisted various other officers within my limited experience. I had tried my best but as I had little knowledge and few skills in this field there were not many job opportunities for which I was proficient.

Essentially, I was doing secretarial duties, and as I did not receive any negative criticism or concerns, I thought my work was acceptable. It came as a dreadful shock to find out at this interview with my supervisors, certain officers had complained about my performance. Newly promoted to Commercial Crime Staff/Sergeant Wray Bradford and Sergeant Adam Storm, my current supervisor, said there were so many mistakes in my work, my accuracy in proof reading statements meant there were not done correctly, and the other officers were not satisfied with my work either. (The mistakes in this book are clearly mine) I could feel my lip tremble with fear and I was taken completely by surprise. I was uncomfortable and the fact my face was turning red may have made them uncomfortable. My supervisors could see from my reaction I was unaware of any problems. I explained no one had mentioned dissatisfaction with the work which had been assigned to me. The officers in Commercial Crime who had criticized my work were unaware of my history and did not realize my education and investigative abilities had not been allowed to develop due to the six-year absence. Everyone, just as lost as me.

I tried to make a joke of it in my attempt to regain my composure: "Well, guys, at least I was consistent in my mistakes. I made the same ones for everyone." I started to chuckle and this lightened the atmosphere. I thanked them for bringing this issue to my attention and asked what I needed to do in order rectify the situation. They were surprised and offered suggestions, bearing in mind my limited ability.

However, I began to see the pattern developing. My history with the RCMP did not allow for a trusting relationship and now I felt I was being 'set up' to fail and possibly get fired. I made this feeling known to the D Division Representative Sergeant Craig Noman, Stanley Smith of Employee Services, and my lawyer. It seemed like history was repeating itself and I was terrified. My mind was clouded. Could I go through this again? I knew I needed to protect myself and continued to take notes regarding my duties and documented conversations with officers on the payment of the legal and school fees and the 'accommodation' process.

I tried to keep my composure, but this was difficult. A few days ago, I had just been told that I was going to have to stay in Commercial Crime and now it looked like no one was satisfied with my work. My supervisors also said as I was going to be on Commercial Crime for another two years, they had been 'ordered' to make me a Commercial Crime Officer.

Looking at them both, I calmly said, "You can order me to take courses related to Commercial Crime, but I will not willingly take courses in an area in which I have no knowledge, skills or interest. I have been lied to by Staffing. I plan to see the new Staffing Inspector to rectify this situation as soon as possible."

From my perspective, I did not take what my supervisors had said as a punishment. They were following orders to make me a Commercial Crime investigator. No one in Staffing was listening to my supervisors and no one was listening to me. Up to this point my supervisors had been supportive and continued to be sympathetic in my quest to get out of Commercial Crime. However, I did agonize about the future of my career. I hated my job in Commercial Crime, it was humiliating, and the jobs assigned were, in my opinion, demeaning considering my skills. This situation was not an 'accommodation' from the very beginning and I believed the harassment and discrimination was continuing from high-ranking officers within the RCMP in D Division. The staff I worked with on Commercial Crime were great, but I simply could never be an operational officer because of the lack of specialized education and investigative experience over the previous seven years, required in Commercial Crime. Sometimes when I drove to work in the morning, during that hour-long drive, I would hope for the miracle of getting out of the section before I became too overwhelmed. Somehow, I managed to keep coming to work in spite of how I felt about the whole 'accommodation' process. I refused to give up.

After the meeting with my supervisors, I truly felt like I had been slammed to the mat from all sides. I wanted to speak to the officers who, behind my back, were not pleased with my work, yet did not tell me. After completing a task, I would ask the officer, "if there is anything missing or wrong let me know." I never got any replies advising me of mistakes. I asked the officers why they did not contact me months ago regarding the mistakes I had made, and further explained the recent return to police duties. Again I clarified my limited experience in this area and the need for guidance as to the proper completion of forms and other duties.

One evening I overheard Chief/Superintendent B Crusoe remark to Inspector Victor Belling, of Commercial Crime, that "She is the Princess of Darkness." They were talking about me. I had sent an email, in error, to several senior officers regarding the payment of legal/school fees, and had to quickly retract noting the error, as the email needed to be edited. Chief/Superintendent B. Crusoe had walked into the office and directly into Inspector Victor Belling's office. I passed him by the secretary's desk and he looked angry. I was embarrassed about the error and having sent it, then angry at his comments. However, I let it slide for the moment as I had too much on my mind.

While working in Commercial Crime, I had kept in contact with Stanley Smith from Employee Services whom I had met back in September 2002 when we had discussed my return to work. I also emailed or faxed copies of letters to my lawyer on the concerns of the 'accommodation', the RCMP's failure to find a suitable position and failure to pay the school and legal fees as promised in November 2002. The response to my emails to Stanley Smith, or Sergeant Fauxl or Sergeant Lucas on these issues was always the same, 'to wait and see', or 'a decision is forthcoming.' No decision was ever received. I received lawyer's bills for work being done for me during the last few months and forwarded these to Sergeant Fauxl, who was supposed to be handling the payment. He promptly returned them, telling me he was not authorized to pay these bills. I could not get a straight answer from him nor from Training Branch.

Next day I sent the following email to Stanley Smith office: "I was wondering why I was never considered for a newly created position called Workforce Engagement/Wellness Initiative. Would this have not been an ideal area where my input would be beneficial?" I had been told by Stanley Smith that Assistant Commissioner Thomas Smith had a feeling that there might be a bad influence on other officers I was in contact with as a result of my experiences. This, he said, was the reason given by Assistant Commissioner Smith why no effort was made to move me into a more suitable position. I challenged this assumption on two grounds: (1) Assistant Commissioner Thomas Smith had never spoken to me since my return to work on my current 'accommodation' on Commercial Crime and 'a feeling' is neither an accurate nor a qualified assessment; (2) at no time during my return to work has my behavior or work ethic been anything but positive and professional in all duties assigned, and a willingness to make this 'accommodation' work. Any issues with my work are due to the fact I was held back for years and did not have the education or experience necessary to be on Commercial Crime. The RCMP was unlawfully trying to medically discharge me.

I was notified by Tim Skavinski the Commissioner would look at my grievance on November 20th, 2003 unless he had competing issues to deal with. What could be more 'competing' than a trip to Canadian Human Rights and a lawsuit from me? I asked that I be kept informed of any progress or decision regarding my school and legal fees.

The RCMP was making it difficult for me to want to remain an employee. One can only interpret the motives. I had a meeting with my lawyer, Roger, to have him send another letter to the Commissioner to explain I have not been 'accommodated'. The letter was sent in late November. The Commissioner had wanted updates on my situation and status every few months regarding his decision of August 2002, to order D Division to accommodate me according to the RCMP policy. I felt the messages he was getting from D Division were misleading. The responses from the officers in D Division had indicated I was 'accommodated', and I felt quite sure that was the message being conveyed to Ottawa. I sent an email to the Assistant Commissioner asking for his help in being assigned to another position. However his email response was: 'Have an interview with the new Staffing Officer, Inspector Ezra Adder.' I made arrangements to see this Inspector early in January of 2004. Another Christmas went by and I was still on Commercial Crime. I was not excited knowing that I could very well be in this same position for the next two years. At home, we managed to have fun and enjoy our time off.

During my quest to get the money for the legal and school fees and secure another more suitable position, I sent emails to our Division Representative Sergeant Craig Noman, Stanley Smith and copied them to my lawyer. It appeared that Staffing had decided not to take any action on any of the issues regarding my requests.

I spent two days preparing for the interview with Inspector Adder. I researched all our policies on members with disabilities, duty to accommodate, discrimination in the work place, directives, labour laws, everything related to my situation. I prepared it in an easy-to-understand format so I could explain to Inspector Adder why leaving me in Commercial Crime was a violation of our own policies. I went in to meet with him and spent the better part of ninety minutes explaining and showing him pages from the documents, RCMP regulations and policies I had researched and printed out. At the end of my presentation, he said I reminded him of his daughter. I thought to myself, 'This is not relevant to my presentation but so what if I did remind him of his daughter? He said he would have to get back to me and I would know shortly. I left his office with renewed hope of getting out of Commercial Crime and on with my career. Looking back, I was able to see how easily the RCMP had shuffled my hopes back and forth like a cat playing with mouse before killing it.

I waited several weeks before I received the dreaded email from Inspector Adder in January 2004. He decided I was best suited in Commercial Crime and could apply for any other position for which I fit the medical profile. Anyone might wonder if I was being "accommodated" in one section, why could I apply for a position not within my medical restrictions? All the officers I had spoken with about the "accommodation" and the payment of school and legal fees simply refused to help, and were not up front about who would be making decisions or where could I go for redress. This type of harassment is abuse of power.

For the next several months I sent emails and made phone calls to Sergeant Fauxl, Stanley Smith and Sergeant Craig Noman regarding the payment of school and legal fees. I was extremely frustrated with the run-around I was getting from these officers. No one was willing to give me an answer about when I would receive payment. Finally, I decided to send a short email to the Commissioner on the matter. The next day I was called to Chief/Superintendent Crusoe's office on the fourth floor. He looked like a short version of the MASH character, Frank Burns, with a moustache. He wanted to know why I had sent the email and if I wanted help, I should not have sent emails out of the Division without first speaking to him. I described my situation with the 'accommodation' process and the difficulties in Commercial Crime, the non-payment of legal and school fees, which had been agreed upon in September of 2002 prior to my return to work.

He said, "I should not let the small amount of money, (which amounted to about $14,000) affect the happiness of my career in the RCMP."

My mind was racing, as I did not know what message he was giving me. Maybe $14,000.00 was not much money to him but it sure as hell was a lot of money to me. Since his salary far out-reaches that of a Constable, I felt he had no right to pass any judgment.

He said he would look into my 'accommodation' and get back to me. At this point I felt it was just more lip service, but willing to give him a chance. I thought D Division would be capable of creative ideas, again I was wrong. This man was being creative in wanting to get me out of the RCMP. Nothing was done from his office, however, he did suggest I make myself more willing to transfer to another province. The male officers who had been 'accommodated' in the RCMP did not have to uproot their families and move so I refused. Once again I could see the waves of discrimination and abuse rolling towards me.

I documented everything and prepared a grievance for the delay in paying my legal and school fees. My lawyer sent letters to Ottawa outlining how I was not being 'accommodated' in Commercial Crime as per our own RCMP policy, by reason of the various clerical duties being assigned to me. A letter was sent to me from the Commissioners' representative concluding I was, in fact, "accommodated" in Commercial Crime and the RCMP had fulfilled its duty to "accommodate" injured officers in the RCMP. Can anyone read in this organization?

This issue was becoming an unending nightmare. Because of all my hard work, the lengthy grievances and resulting changes in policies, I was still being discriminated against, suffering under continued harassment and as a result of abuse of power on the part of the RCMP, being forced to stay in a position that I could not do. Nothing had really changed from 1996, the beginning of my six years in the grievance process.

There is nothing in RCMP policies to say Constables cannot speak to the Commissioner. There is, however, a proper chain of command. For example, I would speak to my supervisor about a concern, and if not satisfied, go to the Inspector in charge of the section; if still not satisfied, I could go up the ranks to the Superintendent, then the Commanding Officer of the Division, Assistant Commissioner Thomas Smith. It was winter 2004 and nothing was happening. In March of 2004, I gave up on D Division. I prepared a lengthy email to the Commissioner of the RCMP explaining exactly what had been occurring in the "accommodation" process, the failure to pay the legal and school fees and the continued abuse. It took many hours of preparation as I wanted to explain the facts and who in D Division had not made any effort to rectify the situation.

After several weeks of preparation of the email, I copied my letter and gave it to my supervisors, Stanley Smith and Sergeant Craig Noman, advising them this was a rough copy of what I intended sending, except it had not yet been edited. I prepared the final draft which I sent the following morning, knowing full well the result could go two ways: either the RCMP would move me to a suitable position or the RCMP would refuse to do anything and continue with the abuse. I decided that whatever happened, doing something was better than doing nothing.

This is a copy of the information which I sent to the Commissioner of the RCMP on April 13, 2004. I stated the facts, just the facts.

Dear Sir:

As a result of your decision on my Medical Discharge Grievance, August 28, 2002, D Division was ordered to accommodate me. I returned to work after a six year fight to remain a member of the RCMP in D Division. Your decision required the settling of several outstanding issues. Most of these issues have yet to be resolved. It appears that my request for assistance falls on deaf ears. It is my belief that this resistance can be viewed as discriminatory in nature. I feel that I have been more than reasonable, and that fifteen months delay would be seen by an outside authority as unreasonable in nature.

Once your decision was received by D Division, a meeting was set up between myself and the Employee Service Manager, Stanley Smith in September 2002. There were concerns of certain issues that should be resolved prior to my returning to work. My concern was that once I was working, nothing would be resolved and this is exactly what has occurred. Since my return to work, I have had to devote hours and hours everyday to dealing with trying to determine the status or why delays are happening. As a result, I have been sending hundreds of emails, letters in attempts to resolve the issues listed in letter September 2, 2002, as the following:

1. The return of my badge. (received my first day.)

2. Payment of legal and school fees for the six year grievance. Dur-

ing the six year grievance process, I completed two diplomas at my own expense in the Human Resource field. I was training myself for a non–operational position, in anticipation of hoping to have continued employment in the RCMP. I was told that the RCMP will not pay for school fees if a member is on administration duties or being medically discharged. I received a letter of denial indicating I was discharged from the force in 1999. This was completely in error, as I was discharged wrongfully only from December 1 to 23, 1999 when I was informed by Pay Section that I was reinstated with full benefits. Why does staffing in D Division have so much erroneous information on my situation?

I was forced to hire counsel as I was told that I would receive no assistance from the RCMP. Section 47.1(1) of the RCMP Act and the Commissioner's Standing Orders (grievances) require entitled members to a Force-paid lawyer. I was never offered that option. Therefore, I view a denial of reimbursement as discrimination in nature under the Canadian Human Rights.

3. A position where my knowledge, skills and interests could best be used to serve the force while maintaining dignity in the workplace as per our policy. The many positions identified were listed in a letter to Stanley Smith, September 2002, as he was acting on behalf of A/Comm. Thomas Smith. I have since added other sections that my training could be used. However, all requests have been denied. I am currently in a position that does not allow me advancement under my special circumstances. The attempt for six years to dismiss me as a member has irreparably harmed my career progression.

4. Willingness to transfer to another division so I can maintain a successful and rewarding career in my chosen field.

All these were agreed upon and I was reassured that a position fitting my knowledge, skills and interest would be found. It came as quite a surprise when the job offered was in Commercial Crime, a section I never indicated any interest and in which I have no knowledge, training or skills. Yet I was ordered, in November 2002, by A/Comm. Smith, to *attend Commercial Crime Section (CC). This was strange. However, I attended and performed to the best of my abilities in all duties assigned. My supervisors have been supportive of my limitations but realize that this is not a good fit.*

In December 24, 2002, I spoke to Sgt. Front, (Staffing) and addressed my concern that I am not qualified for Commercial Crime. I inquired as to the attempts Staffing was making in trying to find a better suited position. He suggested that I need to prove myself for six months and then the situation would be reviewed. At that time I felt there was hope for a career that had my knowledge, skill and interest. I continued to work and perform to the best of my limited knowledge, skills and interest. Many of the duties were clerical in nature. My supervisor and peers were pleased with my positive attitude and strong work ethic. However, it was and continues to be difficult to assign duties that are not clerical in nature and I have no qualifications, skills in this area. The investigative skills necessary come from years of being an operational officer. Something that I have been denied as a result of the six year grievance.

After six months, June 2003, I spoke again with Sgt. Front who advised me that I was to remain on Commercial Crime Section for another two years. This was mystifying to me and my supervisors. I contacted the CO A/Comm. Smith who then suggested I contact Insp. Adder Staffing Officer. Insp. Adder and I met in early December 2003. I had hoped that he would see that the position on CC was not working out for both myself and the rest of the CC staff. He suggested that I apply for all jobs that I am medically fit to perform but I am to remain in Commercial Crime. How can I apply for any position when I am being accommodated in CC? This is frustrating.

Legal and School Fees: I waited for my legal and school fees during the first few weeks of my return to work, November 2002. I forwarded a few emails and letters but was advised that a decision on payment was not required and had to come from Ottawa. The decision denying reimbursement came from Supt. Jerry Kayen, NW Region, Human Resources

*on February 27, 2004. That decision took over fourteen months to ar-
rive. Hundreds of emails had been sent from Craig Noman (Div Rep)
and myself between Supt. Kayen and Sgt. Fauxl. After each conversation
we were left with the impression that an answer would be given shortly.
I have forwarded a grievance for payment of legal fees. An email was
also sent to Dept Comm. Smith on this issue requesting that my case be
viewed as the special circumstances dictate.*

*This date, I received a letter denying reimbursement of school fees.
Again, it has taken over fourteen months to arrive. The impression that I
and others who counseled me arrive at, is that this was being deliberately
delayed. I shall be deciding on what course of action to continue.*

*In closing, is seems that after this six year grievance, recommen-
dations from the External Review Board and finally your decision, it
should have been made very clear that my situation has special/unique
circumstances and therefore, treated as such. Instead, Sir, the only issues
addressed, have been the return of my badge and I was given a desk,
but not a desk in an area that I have any qualification, training skills or
interest.*

*Those with whom I consult within D Division and I can only make
two assumptions: there is an inability to recognize my situation in regards to the above noted as not fitting in the guidelines therefore being
refused; OR the alternative this present situation screams retribution for
my fighting to remain in the RCMP and to be treated in an equal and
fair manner. This again is in violation of the Canadian Human Rights
Act. All other issues that had been agreed upon by agents acting on the
CO's behalf have not been met. I can only react to my history with the
RCMP. I feel that once again I am being sexually discriminated against.
Returning to work in November 2002, gave me hope to believe there was
future for me in the RCMP. A career where my knowledge, skills training and interest could best be used for the force. Regrettably, it has been
made clear that is not the case.*

On April 5, 2004, I spoke with C/Supt. B. Crusoe on the above not-

ed. He was unable to comment on payment of legal and school fees as he indicated he may be the adjudicator on Level l grievance. He wondered, as to the fourteen month delay in a decision being forwarded to me. He indicated that there were not other positions available due to the north south rotation and perhaps if I offer to transfer anywhere in Canada, a more suitable position could be found. This was not mentioned in November 2002 when I was to return or in your decision of August 28, 2002. My husband is in the military and cannot go anywhere in Canada. If I was to transfer across Canada, there are a limited number of divisions where it would be suitable. I find the lack of creative thinking in my accommodation process pathetic. I have much to offer the RCMP and had hoped my training and talents would be considered in placing me.

I write to you Sir, as my last resort to solve this situation inside the organization. D Division and the NW Region are to date, refusing to fulfill recommendations made by you in dealing with the special circumstances. I am being forced to train in an area that I have absolutely no training, skills or interest or hope of ever advancing my career. The people who transfer into Commercial Crime have advanced investigative experience, University training and choose this section. My opinion has never been considered in placement. Thank you for your time.

Cst. Sherry Lee Benson-Podolchuk

I also prepared and forwarded two grievances, one for the school fees and the other for the legal fees. In my mind if D Division was going to play tough, then so was I. The grievance process had changed from thirty-three different stages to three, which encouraged early resolution of a grievance. I held my breath for the response from D Division.

Retribution From Within

THE REACTION WAS SWIFT. THE NEXT MORNING, Sergeant Craig Noman, the Division Rep, stormed into my office and started yelling at me, calling me a liar and untrustworthy. I was stunned at the threat from the person elected by the officers of D Division to represent us and protect us. I could not understand his childish behavior. Is this how a representative of the officers of the RCMP handles a difficult situation, with name-calling and running away without trying to understand the entire incident? If there is one thing I value in myself it is the fact that I am honest. I admitted I sent the letter and further added I had told all parties who received a copy yesterday, it was not edited but the letter would be sent.

He went on and on about how I had said I wouldn't send the letter to the Commissioner and did anyway. How could I be trusted? I sat in silence not knowing what he was talking about. I tried to remind him that I had given him a rough draft and not the final copy of my letter to the Commissioner. He obviously did not seem to understand and flatly refused to listen. Craig had been in the office of Chief/Superintendent Crusoe trying to negotiate the payment of my school and legal fees when Crusoe showed him the letter on the email from the Commissioner (who apparently was furious at D Division for not handling the situation properly). Craig stormed out of Crusoe's office and came directly to see me. He also said my name was on the letter, not his.

He warned, "You think you are happy now, photocopying, I can tell you that they won't do anything for you, all requests will be put on 'ignore'. I can't trust you and will put on your file that you are untrustworthy. You will have to ask someone else for help. I won't help you. Maybe one of the sub-reps". After he left, I documented his outrage in my notebook.

Craig was blowing this all out of proportion and flatly denied I had spoken to him about the copy. Later that day I spoke with Stanley Smith, my Supervisor, and Inspector Victor Belling who did not get confused about what I had said the previous day regarding the unedited copy. They fully understood the edited letter was to be sent the following day. There was no misunderstanding by either of them and they were not upset.

The first time I met Insp. Victor Belling, in December of 2002, when he arrived to take over as Officer in Charge of Commercial Crime, he said, "I understand what has happened and that you have to do what you feel is necessary to do. I only ask you keep me in the loop," which I did while I was on Commercial Crime and I continued to send him copies of emails.

My concern was if I got no support from the Division Representative, where could I expect support. Once again, the Tisdale nightmare seemed to unfold. Inspector Belling suggested I lie low for a while and show the RCMP I wanted to belong. I wondered, 'What does that look like?' I was scared. I was nervous about the letter and the potential fallout directed at me and, judging from Craig's reaction, I had reason to be scared. I had difficulty sleeping, concentrating and working at D Division. The RCMP is known for idle chitchat about each other and the local rumours. I knew it would not take long for the news about my letter to spread through the building where I worked. I had become accustomed to the coffee chat on a daily basis but I got tired of the judging and negative comments about people I knew and liked. For example, while walking by a table in the cafeteria one day, I overheard an officer quietly say to another person, "She's the trouble maker…" My first reaction was to run and hide. Instead I stopped, turned to the table and smiled, "Good morning, such a lovely day." I looked directly at the man who spoken and stared him straight in the face. I felt empowered when he looked down at his plate.

I had counted on my husband David's support while I had been preparing the letter to the Commissioner and trusted his judgment. He gave me comfort and strength in preparing and sending it. His kind words kept me grounded: "Remember, sweetie, you didn't do anything wrong."

I had to remind myself of this daily. I was afraid and did not like going to a place I hated and was frightened. I talked to my therapist about how I should deal with these feelings and how to continue to work. She reminded me that it is okay to be afraid each time we stand up for ourselves in a new situation. This was new to me. I don't think anyone in the history of the RCMP had jumped over so many heads to get to the Commissioner.

Over the next two weeks I frequently saw Craig in the cafeteria or hallway. I would smile and say "Hello." Most times, if there was no one else around, he did not acknowledge me. I found his attitude was unprofessional. As a police officer there were many situations where I was called upon to assist the public and did not like the person I was dealing with, yet, I performed my duties to the best of my abilities and did not allow personal bias to affect my work ethic. This was not the case with some of the officers involved in my situation over the years. I was getting no job satisfaction at work and becoming increasingly depressed with Staffing ignoring and avoiding my requests on the accommodation issue. These senior officers let their personal biases affect their judgment in handling the grievance and the 'accommodation' process.

I spoke with my boss, Inspector Belling, regarding the reaction I got from the Division Representative and asked what kind of further reaction I could expect from the officers who had been mentioned in my letter. Inspector Belling then told me that Chief/Superintendent Crusoe came down to see him shortly after the incident with Craig, and referred to the letter I sent to the Commissioner. Crusoe was waving a copy of my letter, shouting, 'Look what she did.'

Inspector Belling had replied, "Yes, she did, and were you listening to her, was anyone?" He added, "It was professionally put together." Inspector Belling was not at all upset about the letter and thanked me for keeping him informed. He knew my issues with the 'accommodation' situation had nothing to do with the Commercial Crime Section.

The next few weeks went by without incident. Occasionally I saw Craig Noman in the cafeteria or hallway and he would not initiate a "Hello."

Early in April 2004, I received a call from Superintendent Kayen, Human Resource Office, North West Region, Regina, Saskatchewan, who wished to discuss my letter and requested a meeting with me in a few days. I agreed. When we met a few days later, I again hoped that my situation at work would change. Superintendent Kayen quickly agreed I should be reimbursed for my legal and school fees and we agreed on an amount. Although I had paid $4,400 for all the school fees and $14,000 in legal fees, I agreed to settle for much less. He told me I could only claim for legal fees directly related to the Medical Discharge. In other words, legal help prior to my being served the Notice of Discharge back in November 1999, could not be reimbursed. This was better than nothing and I was completely overwhelmed with mental fatigue and the stress was depressing me. Superintendent Kayen told me I would have my money within a couple of weeks, but I had to sign a legal agreement indicating the grievance was over. As long as I got my money and was 'accommodated' into a position utilizing my knowledge, skills and interest as well as maintaining dignity in the work place, then fine, I would sign. I received a copy of the legal agreement by email, printed it off and had my Supervisors witness my signature. This copy was sent to Superintendent Kayen in Regina and I received my money in June of 2004. I paid off the remainder of my legal bill and put some money away for my daughter's university.

Superintendent Kayen suggested I take an Occupational Work Assessment to determine the type of position best suited to my knowledge, skills, interest and abilities. I readily agreed. He was concerned no effort had been made to do this Work Assessment prior to my return to duty. He also asked if I was being harassed. By that time, I had been abused for so many years by RCMP organization and harassment and discrimination almost seemed natural. I could not readily identify the exploitation. He looked relieved when I answered "No." Eventually, upon completion of the RCMP Harassment Workshop the following month, was able to recognize it as abuse. The Harassment Workshop was a course I had wanted to take upon my arrival to Commercial Crime in 2002 however, more senior officers were scheduled to take it first.

At this Workshop, we had to talk about a work-related incident, which could be considered "harassment." I had so many situations I wanted to share. The other participants were stunned with my narrative of the 'abuse' I had endured. I left the Workshop feeling demoralized. Superintendent Kayen had the training in this area as the Human Resource Officer for Manitoba, yet he had said nothing. At this time I had come to realize that when a person is subjected to abuse for a long time, they do not think anything is wrong and therefore allow it to continue. To me it was like a person in an abusive relationship.

The violence continues, and slowly over time, it escalates. The person in the relationship, in many cases, cannot see something is wrong. For these reasons, this is why I kept trying to improve my situation without going outside the RCMP. I had thought other officers that were treated poorly also sent letters, emails and grievances according to procedure in the RCMP.

During that summer I went to work with the renewed hope of having a new position. I was notified that the Occupation Work Assessment would be done in Winnipeg. There were several meetings with the psychologist who explained the importance of the various tests and questionnaires which I was required to complete. These were meant to determine my knowledge, skills and areas of interest. The process took several months from the first meeting in September 2004 to January 2005, when the report was submitted to Dr. Sue Jupe, Health Officer for the RCMP. I felt comfortable with the psychologist and was aware he would be able to assist in having me assigned to a new position. The psychologist had indicated at our first meeting, September 23, 2004 he would send me a copy of his final report and if I did not agree then he would make the changes prior to sending it to Dr. Jupe. Only the recommendations were to be sent to Staffing, all other information was confidential.

By the middle of November the Occupational Testing had been completed and all that was left to do was wait, wait and wait. The report did not arrive until early January 2005. I was able to give input on the report with regard to some changes in the language. I did not want the RCMP to think I did not have an ideal childhood. In my opinion some of the tests did not make a lot of sense, but then I am not the expert. Finally, in the report, it was put in writing, 'I was not suited for Commercial Crime', but best suited for the positions I had previously identified in 2002. These being; Staffing and Personnel Career Management, Ethics Advisor, Instructor-Trainer, General Administrator, Human Resource Management, Alternate Dispute Resolution/

Wellness Coordinator, Women's Issues Advisor and Human Rights/ Equity Coordinator. I was livid and discouraged at the time wasted while I had to endure working at Commercial Crime. My career delayed another two years because of the RCMP's refusal and failure to 'accommodate'.

I was anxious for the report to be forwarded to D Division so I could be moved to a more suitable position and perhaps catch up on my career. However, this would never happen. It took a car accident to make me realize I was never going to have a fulfilling career with the RCMP.

In April 2005, I sent an email to Supt. Kayen, to thank him for getting things moving with regard to finding a more suitable position for me within the RCMP. I knew the only reason he was agreeing to pay the fees was due to the letter I had sent to the Commissioner.

I felt less anxious about having sent the letter to the Commissioner after meeting with Supt. Kayen as he was also willing to move ahead with the "accommodation issue." I still felt I needed to prove myself a worthy officer of the RCMP and went to speak with Inspector Victor Belling, the Officer in Charge of Commercial Crime. I needed to demonstrate my commitment to having a career within the RCMP. I asked myself, 'How do I show the RCMP I want to have a career and I am not a risk?' It was easy; all I had to do was go to the RCMP Regimental Dinner that was coming up on April 16th at D Division.

I bought a ticket and planned to attend. Months earlier I had ordered three star badges to put on my dress uniform, the ceremonial red serge. I wanted to proudly display the years of service. Each star has five points which represent the number of years of service. As I now had 16 years, I could sew on three stars. I was so proud to go to the dinner. It was the first RCMP function I had attended since October of 1999.

On April 16 2005, my daughter Nadine and I drove to the city for several purposes, including house hunting with her father, John, shopping for clothes and for me to attend the regimental dinner. While I was at the RCMP dinner, Nadine had dinner with John. The tables were set up in two long rows and a head table. The men and women naturally gravitated to their separate sides. I sat on the side with the men. I knew if I sat with the women, only a few of the loud officers would dominate the entire night's conversation. It had been my experience at these types of dinners some officers like to dominate the conversation by speaking loudly, and go on and on about all their accomplishments. Sitting across from me was an American Customs Officer. On each side of me were younger officers with less service in the RCMP. They asked how much service did I have and were surprised at my answer of 'sixteen years.' They were more surprised when I related some of my not-so-pleasant experiences with D Division. At that point, our section of the table began a conversation on how the RCMP fails its officers. It was suggested by one of the younger men, I run for the Division Representative position, and by using my own experiences help other officers. I felt proud and yet a sense of gloom, knowing some senior officers who were less than cooperative, would keep me from being successful. Yet, wondering, "should I try." This was great because the people serving the food were, in fact, Inspectors. I had a great time speaking with these men and was pleased to be a part of the evening. Once again I had renewed hope of belonging.

After the dinner and some short speeches, I left for home. At 10:00 p.m. Nadine and I drove back to Winnipeg Beach laughing and talking about the wonderful day. We had found a condominium to buy for Nadine, she had had a great dinner with her father and I had enjoyed my dinner. Nadine did not have her full license and needed experience driving at night. Things were about to change.

Hanging On By My Fingernails, Don't Ask Me To Salute

THE NIGHT SKY WAS BLACK WITH NO MOON. THREE miles north from the turn-off road to our house, a large deer stood on the left shoulder of the southbound lane on Highway 8. All I saw was the whiteness of the lifted tail and the grey fur blending in with the road. Nadine and I both saw the deer at the same time and she made a controlled deceleration. Suddenly the deer jumped in front our car and was struck full-length, the deer blew apart from the impact.

The force of the collision threw the deer onto the opposite shoulder. Blood was everywhere and the front hood and lights smashed. We had no lights now but managed to drive home with the four-way flashers. The sight of the deer guts on the front of the car was very traumatic for Nadine. I drove the last few miles while she phoned the police. My neck felt tight however, at the time I did not feel any pain. I was so thankful Nadine was not hurt other than the shock. The next day was a different story for me, beginning with increased stiffness and pain in my neck and back. By the second evening, the pain in my neck and back became severe to the point where any movement in my neck made me instantly nauseated.

A visit to the doctor's office on Monday confirmed I had whiplash and a sprained back, so for the next few weeks I was off work. I could barely move or turn my head, and sleep was impossible. I lay on the couch for a couple of weeks fading in and out of restless sleep. Family members took turns driving me to physiotherapy appointments and delivering groceries. David was not around to help because he had flown to Chile for three weeks with the military. He had left two days prior to the accident.

He called several times to check on my progress: he said, "It is difficult to be so far away when you are in pain." I assured him all I was doing was taking anti-inflammatory pills and sleeping. The Manitoba Public Insurance agent came to my home and gave me much needed advice and assistance during my injury. A rehabilitation nurse also came to discuss different types of brooms and other aids to make house work manageable. I could not sweep the floor without feeling sick. The neck injury made me woozy. This benefit from Manitoba Public Insurance was new for me and I was thankful for their assistance.

Nadine would get up and go to school and I would remain lying down. She would come home and I would still be lying down. With her graduation coming in just a couple of months I hoped I would be able to attend without my neck collar. The only energy I had was to wash myself and brush my teeth. I needed help dressing. I could not move my arms over my head.

After three weeks of being a lump with a heating pad on the couch, I took a good look in the mirror and noticed my hair was getting long. I decided this was something positive.

Nadine responded to my attitude: "Mom, you are certainly a glass is more than half-full person".

I had to laugh. The inactivity and the lack of being able to exercise frustrated me. Exercise had been part of my life since I was twelve years old. It was even difficult to hold a book to read or to sit at the computer or bake. I have always enjoyed all these pastimes. Now I had to wait to gather mobility and endurance before I could even start the recovery process. I found it exasperating.

I went to physiotherapy for several weeks after my accident and slowly my physical stamina improved to the point where I was able to be more active. Upon David's return at the end of April, I was greatly improved. After three months I found great pleasure in baking cookies although I had to lie down between batches and rest. The road to recovery was long. As the weather in May improved so did my ability to sit up for longer periods of time. But I still could not drive my standard vehicle forward, let alone turning to back out of the garage and Nadine still did not have her license. As June approached, I worried about being able to help Nadine pick out her dress for graduation. Sharing in this event was important to both Nadine and I.

My sister Kim, Nadine and I took a trip to Winnipeg in search of items for Nadine's graduation. I was very proud of Nadine and her dedication to school work, so it was exciting to watch her up on the stage during her graduation, yet sitting for the lengthy ceremony required pain killers. However, I had taken my trusty neck brace to the reception for added support.

As July approached my health improved. Eventually I was able to return to work on a new program that the RCMP had implemented, Graduated Return to Work. In 2002 this position was in the developmental stage. This time, I was assured that 'this job was perfect for someone like me.' The officer in charge of the Member Employee Assistant Program, MEAP, knew what type of experience was needed to help other officer's deal with discrimination and grievances. He was confident that once the job was advertised I would be sure to get it. Once again I was filled with hope. The Return to Work was the rebundling of duties that our Administration policy, Duty to Accommodate Members with Disabilities, and the Commissioner's Standing Orders outlines:

1. The RCMP recognizes that the Duty to Accommodate facilitates a member's right to continue to work and to maintain employment status when there is conflict between the member's need and the terms and conditions of employment.

2. The RCMP will accommodate members with disabilities up to the point where this may cause undue hardship for the RCMP. The Supreme Court of Canada has stated that some hardship is acceptable.

2a. Some of the factors which may constitute undue hardship include: financial cost, impact on a collective agreement, employee morale problems, interchangeability of the workforce and facilities, size of the employer's operations and safety. The impact will depend on the circumstances of each case.

3. The RCMP can justify a discriminatory employment practice or rule, if it can establish a bona fide occupational requirement. For the purpose of employment equity see # 2.

4. Through cooperation and consultation, it is the responsibility of management, Staff Relations Representatives and members with accommodation needs to identify, implement and support appropriate accommodation initiatives.

4a. Successful accommodation requires the support and commitment of everyone in the workplace. All employees are expected to assist and support accommodation initiatives.

Rebundle – means that existing positions will be re-examined to determine if they can be restructured or modified into a new bundle of duties which would allow a person to work within his/ her limitations.

The RCMP's definition of accommodation read 'the design and adaptation of the work environment to the needs of as many types of persons as possible.' According to the Supreme Court of Canada, accommodation is what is required in the circumstances of each case to avoid discrimination.

The RCMP Career Manager will: 'At the request of the Return to Work Facilitator/Delegate, interview the affected member to establish his/her career profile, e.g. updated resume, education, knowledge, skills and abilities, work experience, career goals and interests, training needs and desire to be accommodated.'

On paper the Commissioner and delegates appear to have genuine concern for the officers however, enforcing this policy was ineffective. I wonder at how these apparently intelligent individuals could not understand this policy and could clearly dismiss the recommendations made by the Commissioner of the RCMP. As for the new position of Return to Work Coordinator, I had to wait for it to be advertised on the RCMP web site. I truly felt it was a guarantee for me. I got the same assurance from Division Representative Sergeant Craig Noman, Stanley Smith of Employee Services and Harold Front of Staffing. I waited and waited. However, when the position was advertised in 2004, and I applied for it, the job was given to another officer, Wilma Reading. I had made no secret of my desire to work in this area while I was on Commercial Crime. It came as a surprise the very person for whom I was working, as an Assistant in Commercial Crime did not tell me that she, Wilma, was also applying for the job. I was equally shocked when I read she got the position, a promotion from Corporal to Sergeant and currently an Inspector. There was a sense of betrayal because later I learned everyone else on Commercial Crime knew she was also applying but said nothing to me. I would have asked her for help and suggestions on how to prepare for the interview since I had not been familiar with the process and had been away from the RCMP for many years and I had thought she and I were friends. It came as a stark realization my waiting for this position to be advertised and going through the process of the interview was just the RCMP again paying lip service to my requests and needs. This had been just something to keep me 'happy and quiet' from Staffing. For several weeks after notification of her success as job candidate, Wilma, could not look me in the face. Perhaps she was worried I might grieve the decision. I decided to let that one go.

Needless to say, I was disappointed and slowly realized I wanted to move my career towards an area dealing with Ethics and Conflict Resolution. Grieving the lost job would have resulted in delays for me. Although I was disillusioned, I was also tired of putting my neck out to have it chopped off. It was time to re-evaluate my career direction and felt Ethics was an area about which the RCMP knows nothing. The issue which hurt me the most was the fact Wilma, very shortly after taking the position, was promoted. Promotions to higher ranks result in better opportunities in the RCMP, something that I was denied. All around me, other officers were transferring out or into Commercial Crime Section, with many receiving promotions. It was discouraging and I felt stuck.

I had hoped when I returned from my accident the work situation would improve. Often I met with the Return to Work Coordinator, Wilma, to arrange duties on Commercial Crime. The duties were to be within my physical limitations. Again, the RCMP did not take into account the initial shoulder injury, the impact of how this disability affected my life, so why would I have any faith in this new program to do any better? The return to work program included working for a few hours for a couple of days a week and then progressively increasing the hours. The purpose of this program was to get injured officers back to work as quickly as possible in areas that best used their skills. However, in their haste to get the officers back to work, the RCMP neglected to take into account the type of duties assigned and the negative feelings officers suffer of feeling trapped in jobs that are less than satisfying and with no hope of improving the situation.

In August, I returned to Commercial Crime with the guarantee it would be for a 'short term.' I had little faith in this new process because the RCMP had made so many mistakes the last time they tried to 'accommodate' me, but once again I was willing to hope.

Losing Hope

WHEN I RETURNED TO WORK IN AUGUST, I WAS AGAIN stuck doing the same assistant work in Commercial Crime, with some added duties associated with Human Resources in Staffing. These duties included preparing security forms and checks, making phone calls, and checking references on RCMP applicants for both regular and civilian positions. I enjoyed dealing with the public and using the education I had obtained over the last few years. However, when I requested to be accommodated in a full-time position using my skills and knowledge, the Return to Work Coordinator, Sergeant Wilma Reading, refused, saying, "You will be moved to another section once you have returned to full time hours." I did not know how long that would take. I viewed this as another stalling tactic by the RCMP. I thought this is a lack of common sense! My frustration mounted. In public Sergeant Reading would say I was 'accommodated' in Commercial Crime, yet privately admitted "Commercial Crime was not a good fit." I had little confidence in her ability to really assist me in finding a suitable position within the RCMP.

September 2005 came and went and I continued in Commercial Crime. My daughter was in first Year University and enjoying her independence. David was in Halifax working with the military for the winter. I was at home, stuck in a job that had no future and little job satisfaction.

Over the next few months my injury did not improve as quickly as I had hoped. I remained on Commercial Crime and assisted the Staffing section with security checks on applicants. I also did security interviews for civilian positions at D Division. Once again I was given a few crumbs to keep me quiet.

Due to my neck injury, I had difficulties using the computer, and it gave me a headache. I realized it would take a long time to fully recover from this injury. Even today, I continue to have headaches. My head and neck have never returned to normal, nor am I ever pain-free because of the shoulder injury.

Our new Inspector, Devon Simpler, in charge of Commercial Crime Section, arrived while I was off work with my injury, and upon my return, wanted to interview each officer in the section to inquire about the general atmosphere of the office. He was also inquiring about any difficulties or harassment issues. When he asked me about these issues, I said, "I am being harassed but not in this section." His response dumbfounded me, "Well Sherry, I really don't care about what is happening if it is not relating to this section. Any harassment not involving Commercial Crime is not my concern."

I just stared at him and realized I could not count on his support. Therefore, he did not receive any of the correspondence I sent outside the Division or to the Commissioner regarding the failure in the accommodation efforts of D Division. I thought to myself, 'This man needs help in the Human Relations department and the importance of effective communication. His main concern as a new Inspector was a positive image for keeping his section problem free.' The lack of support made me realize that this man was another senior officer I could not depend on for help. I kept him out of the loop.

As the days wore on from fall to winter, I became increasingly restless. The thought of getting up in the morning to drive back and forth to work became more difficult each day. It is hard to explain how depression works; it creeps into your soul, slowly, day after day. I become like a robot and just did the jobs assigned, without question. November 20, 2005 I was especially sad for an entire day as I realized I had been forced to tolerate the 'accommodation' on Commercial Crime for three years. Little by little, my hope for any kind of satisfying career began to fade.

The duties assigned were demeaning and humiliating. For example, in December 2005, one assigned task was to check the vehicle radio inventory for all the cars on Commercial Crime. The cars were in the outdoor parking lot. The effort involved in verifying the serial numbers required the removal of items from the trunk of each car. I was recovering from a neck and back injury but managed to complete the task and prepare the report. As I completed this chore I thought, "There is no way I can keep on doing these boring, humiliating jobs. I don't think I can make it to pension (20 years of service), let alone a twenty-five or thirty year pension!" I felt I was being violated in front of the other officers at D Division, over and over again, day after day. It seemed as though my life was a mess, not only at work but at home.

We had started renovations to our home in October 2005 and although it was exciting, the mess and confusion were not. By early January, the new addition began to take shape, yet the house was in total chaos. I thought back to 2003 and a conversation I had had with the Health Services Officer, Dr. Jupe, and I remembered her saying: "I have been told that you have made it easy for them at D Division in your accommodation."

These words came back to haunt me. At the time I did not understand what 'easy for them' referred to. But now, despair was welling up inside me. Even the thought of Christmas did not excite me.

I spoke with my therapist about the feelings of sadness and despair. Together, we worked on setting up suggestions to make the job situation bearable. What did I need to do to survive this work environment? Again, Tim Horton's and the daily walk for coffee and exercise at home with the stationary bike were suggested, but these were just survival techniques. Imagine having to create survival techniques to save one's sanity at work. This was not good. In spite of a few days of happiness here and there, I knew all this was slowly destroying me. I also knew that when things got really bad I could call my therapist, at any time. My parents and siblings had been supportive in some areas of my life, however, they did not understand the situation, therefore I could not rely on them for support.

Christmas was approaching. It's my favorite season, and I usually had the tree up and decorated by the end of November. However, this year, I waited for Nadine to finish her exams at university in mid-December. Together we put up the tree. Thankfully, I had bought most of the presents prior to December in order to avoid the big crowds and stressful confusion of shoppers. I did not feel any Christmas spirit. Again, I was only acting happy around the people I loved the most. Several days before David arrived home the electrician was working on the electrical panel late into the night. The walls were open planks so limited privacy. I went to bed at eleven thinking the heat would be on very soon. Finally, at two in the morning the electrician said he could not put the heat on because the work was not complete but he would return early the next day. There was no heat on one of the coldest days in December. I nearly froze in bed despite wearing sweats, wool socks, toque, fleece hoodie and covered with two quilts. My back was shaking all night. David came home for a few days and they were wonderful. He could not believe I had been able to sleep in the midst of all the chaos of the house renovations. During Christmas David set up a bed and TV for me in Nadine's old bedroom so I would have some privacy and not be wakened in the early hours by the sound of the power tools. He had no idea the little room was my salvation from the sanity around me, a quiet place, a small cozy place of tranquility. For that I am ever grateful. I should have been happy, but I was not. I found I was avoiding people. I was not myself and did not like these gloom and doom feelings. The inner peace and happiness that had once filled my heart was replaced with hopelessness. When the holidays ended I dreaded returning to work.

Driving in snow for an hour to a job I hated was becoming increasingly difficult. Upon reflection back to those months, I now recognize these feelings were the beginning of a very deep depression, however, at the time I felt I could handle it alone and did not call on my therapist for help, nor speak with friends about my feelings. Functioning like a robot every day, I began to withdraw from my family and friends, I stopped baking and declined social outings, preferring to stay home alone. My excuses were the continued problems with my neck and headaches relating back to the car accident in April 2005.

The only escape I felt from the negative feelings was exercise, so I would use the stationary bike at home, go for walks or to the recreation center in Gimli and use the equipment. I was not my good-humored self with people. I did not want to go out of my way to lend a hand to anyone. I had nothing left to give and the daily grind began to terrify me.

I was sent to a physiotherapist in Selkirk Manitoba as my neck and back continued to give me pain. One morning in late January 2006, as I drove the twenty five miles south to my appointment in Selkirk, I was listening to the news, which I always do in the morning. The sound of the voices was not registering as I was feeling out of touch when suddenly the words of the announcer caught my attention. I turned up the volume to make sure what I had heard was accurate. The announcer spoke of the settlement that a retired female RCMP had received from the Canadian Human Rights Commission for sexual discrimination by the RCMP ten years previous. Her settlement was in the amount of $975,000. My mouth dropped open and I pulled off to the shoulder to listen again and make sure my ears were not playing tricks on me. Yes, I had heard it right. My chest tightened and I burst into tears at this news. After all the years of suffering from the abuse at Tisdale and D Division, the financial burden of legal fees, the mental anguish of the possible loss of employment and hundreds of sleepless nights, the realization came to me like slap in the face. My career was ruined. D Division would never 'accommodate' my injury and I would be further subjected to retribution for the rest of my service. The only 'settlement' I had received for my six year grievance was for the past three years, being forced to work at a job for which I was not qualified nor was I able to be promoted, my role being that of an assistant to other officers. I continued to cry, quietly at first but the pain inside became overwhelming and loud sobs echoed in the vehicle. My breathing was deep and difficult. It was then, at that moment I knew I could not take this situation any longer. I felt like I wanted to die. D Division had refused to move me to another section as punishment for my winning the six year grievance. This was unbelievable, after all the time and effort I had put into the six years' fight to stay in this very organization which was now destroying me. The policy changes in the RCMP were a direct result of the success of my grievance, and here I was, crumbling.

Standing On The Edge
Of The Abyss

I WAS CRYING SO HARD I COULD NOT CATCH MY BREATH. It seemed my eyes could not stop spilling the hot tears which were rolling down my face. I let out the pain for what seemed forever and when I felt empty and rid of it, a new feeling began to creep in. Rage! I asked myself, "what was I doing here, all these years of being treated like dirt, and for what? Getting forced to stay in a position where I have no qualifications or interest, being denied the opportunity to advance and refused the many requests for a transfer out of Commercial Crime. All I could see was no way, no hope of a satisfying career. Being forced to remain in Commercial Crime for as long as the powers want to make me suffer. Why and with no hope of getting anything better? Punished because I defended my injury and stood up to the RCMP. Reprimanded because I demanded to be treated equally in a workplace without harassment or discrimination. This was my crime?" The anger spilled out in a pounding rage as I began hitting the steering wheel, swearing and shouting, "Those bastards, I won't let them kill me! I can't do this anymore. I would rather sell myself on the streets than work for the RCMP!" To drivers going by on the highway, I probably looked like a lunatic. I thought, "I am crazy, crazy to trust the RCMP of D Division again and allow the abuse to continue. Crazy to think being nice and reasonable would help me in dealing with D Division."

I just wanted to make them pay and wanted it all to be over, the pain, the suffering, the profound sadness and hopelessness. I thought, this is the second time I have been brought to the precipice of despair working for the RCMP. I vowed I would never let this happen to me again. I didn't care about financial stability or the pension, I just wanted out. As I stared out the window, the thoughts going through my mind reflected the years I had devoted trying to save my career and now I had the sudden realization it was ruined. There was no hope.

After several minutes I started driving again in order to keep my physiotherapy appointment in Selkirk, then I would go to Winnipeg to work. I am sure my red face and puffy eyes gave me away when I arrived at the physiotherapist, but I did not say a word about my anguish. After the physiotherapy appointment, I drove to work. That entire day I was like a robot, saying hello to people, typing reports and answering emails. I left work thankful for having the next day off. I paced the house for hours that evening and the next day, not able to sit for any length of time, feeling trapped. I left a message for my therapist to call me to set up a time for the following evening. There was urgency in my voice, which she was able to recognize as coming from someone hanging on by her fingernails. She called back and we scheduled an appointment for the next night. This gave me a sense of hope and allowed me to hang on a little longer. Thoughts of going to sleep and never waking up became less overpowering. I was frightened of myself, I was frightened of what was happening to me. I had never thought of myself as being weak and wanting to kill myself. The thoughts were there and I was terrified of being in the bedroom, close to my sleeping pills. Instead of going to bed, I lay on the couch watching TV until exhaustion overcame me. I had to call my therapist, I recognized the urgency. David would freak out if he thought I may be suicidal. He hated seeing me suffer with cramps which would pass but these feelings of hopelessness just went on and on.

I drove to work the next morning with a new sense of purpose: I had to get out or it would kill me. I knew this was true. I did not care about money now. I just knew I had to get out, today. I went to work, packed all my belongings, personal files and pictures, in a brown box, walked over to the office of the Division Representative Sergeant Howard Brandon and dropped into a chair. I took a deep breath and let my anger go: "Howard, I just came to tell you that I am leaving work and will be filing a complaint for sexual discrimination, harassment, abuse of power and failure to 'accommodate' against seven RCMP officers, and I will be filing a lawsuit in Federal Court. These are the names so you might want to give them the 'heads up': Assistant Commissioner Thomas Smith, Inspector Ezra Adder, Chief Superintendent B. Crusoe, Sergeant Craig Noman, Sergeant Harold Front, Sergeant Jake Fauxl and the Commissioner of the RCMP." I took another deep breath.

Howard looked like a deer caught in headlights. He looked at me apologetically: "Well Sherry, I didn't know things were so bad because you did not come to me or say anything." Then I told him under no circumstances would I put up with this abuse another minute. I began my rant, "I've had enough of being treated this way! All the changes in policy, which came about because of my six-year grievance, the hell, have not helped me at all. Others, yes, but not me. I feel I have been more than reasonable in trying to make this 'accommodation' work, always worried about making waves. Did you know I was sexually assaulted by an officer in Selkirk Detachment? It was Larry G! No? Of course not, because I had been brutalized by my last assignment at Tisdale. Who would believe me? I had drinks and went to his house. I am sure I was neither the first nor the last victim of Larry. I came to

Commercial Crime on the promise it was only for a few weeks, but I have been lied to by those who will be mentioned in my complaint. I can't work like this anymore. I just can't stand being stuck in this demeaning job and not using my skills!" I blurted out all my frustration in what seemed one long breath and felt I was about to break down in tears.

Again Howard looked dumbfounded: "I never would have thought that of Larry G. but then one never knows do they? Let me know if there is anything that I can do for you from my side. I'll represent you if you want. If you plan a grievance I can help with that. You never said anything. And you have to do what you think is best."

"Yes, Howard, I never talked to you because the last Representative Craig Noman, turned on me at the first misunderstanding and refused to help me. Not only that, he said I was untrustworthy, which he was going to put on my file and notify other reps not to trust me. How can I ask for help from this office? I had no one to go to. No one!" I paused for a second by the shocked look on his face appeared to be fear. I continued, "Not to worry, your name won't be mentioned but his name will be on my complaint, so you may want to give him the 'heads up'". I took a breath, "You know, I would rather sell myself on the streets than work for the RCMP, because at least I know that I would be getting fucked on my own terms."

Then I told him I would ask for his help, if I needed it. I got up, thanked him and left. "Good luck, Sherry, I understand how the RCMP fails its members," was his only comment. I could only imagine from this last comment that he had probably been subjected to the wrath of the RCMP at some point in his service.

Back in my department, I went to see my boss, Staff/Sergeant Wray Bradford. He looked at me with concern as I entered his office. My face, tight with determination, told him I was leaving and taking a sick day and may not be coming back. I was at my wits' end adding any chance of my having a career had been ruined. He listened intently, and then said, "You know, Sherry, things were moving ahead prior to your accident but after you came back they did not want to do anything but keep you here. I don't understand as there are many different jobs you could do utilizing your skills. Staying in a job that makes you sick is not a good thing. I wish you the best of luck." I felt tears in my eyes as I said, "Thanks, Wray, my complaint against the RCMP will not reflect the officers on Commercial Crime. My complaint is with certain officers and only with them. Jerry Kayen never once inquired about how things were going while I was off because of my accident. What does that say? Thanks, you have been a fine man to work for." He smiled.

Marching back to my office picked up my box and left the building. In my mind, I swore I would never come back to this building to work. Never. As I walked down the stairs clinging to the brown box, I was overwhelmed with excitement and anxiety. On the way to my car decided to stop and speak to Dr. Sue Jupe from the RCMP Health Service Office. I informed her of my decision. She took me upstairs and made some suggestions as to what I might do in the way of options. She also suggested I take some time off to think about what would be best for me in the future, then send a letter to Superintendent Kayen, Human Resource Officer, North West Region in Regina, outlining different alternatives I may have with regard to leaving or staying in order to get my twenty or twenty five year pension. I would have to send these options to Superintendent Kayen. I thanked her for her help and the suggestions on the pension and left with my box.

Taking Back My Power

ON THE DRIVE HOME, I FELT A SENSE OF RELIEF, SOMETHING I had not felt in a very long time. Later in the evening, I had a tearful session with my therapist dealing with the anguish and frustration in coming to this decision, the fear of killing myself, and how close I came to wanting to do it. Talking to her was a release. The next day I told the physician I need time to think about what to do regarding my job, my difficulty sleeping, and the anxiety and depression. He prescribed medication to help me sleep and put me on stress leave for a month.

My husband and family would never be able to understand what was going on inside of me. It was difficult for them to understand when we discussed my frustration at the failure of the "accommodation." Some family members suggested that I "just go to work and pretend to be happy." That advice was not much help. Although I appreciated their attempts, sometimes even educated people can give advice not realistic or helpful, or may even be just stupid. Telling my husband I was afraid to go into my bedroom because I might take more than the prescribed one-a-night sleeping pills, Zipiclon, would terrify him. As it was, he was doing shift work with the military in Halifax, and was also under a great deal of stress. I did not want him worrying about me. I needed to take care of me. There were days when I did not want be alone and yet had no energy to speak with people. I would drive to Gimli, sit in the local coffee shop at the back where I knew I would be safe and not have to interact. That was all I could do at that time. Very slowly, I began to feel safe again with myself and in my home. I will never forget the depths of despair I felt, and how I mentally crawled out to begin the fight.

On occasion I spoke with Nadine's father, Constable John French. He was also going through a stressful time and could relate to the ineptness of the RCMP in D Division.

This was a very lonely period for me. I was afraid to be alone, yet did not want the company of other people. I was forcing myself to get out of the house despite wanting to stay in the safety of isolation. It was important for me to recognize the need to want to be out in the world in order to save my sanity. My home was either a prison or a sanctuary. How I felt during the day would determine whether or not I left the house. This state of affairs went on for several months. Reluctantly, I went on anti-depressants prescribed by my physician with the full intention of going off the medication, Effxor, once I was finished writing this book. After a few weeks, I did notice a difference in my moods and I was able to cope better with the stress.

The RCMP continued to hound me while I was on stress leave. Phone calls would come during the day from the same Inspector who did not want to know about any harassment unless it involved his section. He just wanted to know how much time I needed and when I was returning to work. I started screening my calls. The answering machine became my new best friend. I would wait for a familiar voice before picking up the phone. If it was the Inspector from Commercial Crime, he would be wanting to make sure all reports were sent in promptly to ensure the correct times were added to my leave report. Somehow, I got the feeling that he was more interested in the accuracy of the annual leave report than he was in me. After a month, my physician decided to keep me on stress and medical leave. However, I got the impression he was intimidated by interference from the RCMP Health Service Office who was pressuring me to return to work. The fact my therapist, though not a medical doctor, had also recommended I remain off work, did not help. I knew I could not mentally go into that building. I needed more time to heal and asked to use my holiday time. At least I could be alone to think and recover.

As the phone calls persisted, I thought of the three RCMP officers who in 2004 had killed themselves with their own service weapons. I could understand the hopelessness they must have felt and the lack of caring by their employer, the RCMP. Death had seemed their only option. I shuddered at the thought of how close I had come, for the second time in my 17 years with the RCMP, to want to end my pain. How I wished the RCMP would back off. All I could do was hang on to reality and life. I wondered if I was the only woman in the RCMP who had been so terribly abused and mistreated. I doubted it.

While I was off sick I started writing down my experiences, the bad and good. First it was as therapy, to help rid myself of the pain, anger and shame of these experiences, but then it became a story. As I wrote of the abuse, inequality and the sexual assaults, I found the feelings of despair were fading. By putting these painful experiences on paper, I removed their grip on my soul. I allowed myself to accept responsibility for my mistakes and to eliminate the shame I felt from my rapes. I am private person, and opening up my life for scrutiny was scary. In writing this all down I had, in fact, gathered strength for the next stage and proceeded with the Canadian Human Rights Commission and Federal Lawsuits. I was fortunate to have a cousin who gave great advice about the editing and clarification of the details in my manuscript.

At this same time, I considered my options with regard to continuing to work for the RCMP, and prepared a report which I sent to Supt. Kayen in Regina. My current options included working in Staffing, doing security checks in recruiting, the Alternative Dispute Resolution Section and retiring at 20 years. I was lucky to have a wonderful, adoring husband who listened to me as I weighed my options. David's support was so important during the entire crisis. I never referred to my suicidal thoughts with David; rather, I would tell him I was having a hard time dealing with work, so he made a special effort to come home every six weeks.

My decision to continue working with the RCMP changed after I spent a week in Mexico with my sister and two other girl friends (who my father humorously called the 'Goodbye Girls' as they had all left their husbands). While in Mexico, I had a hard time relaxing for the first couple of days. It was difficult to let go and relax after being under extreme stress for months. I enjoyed the water and allowed myself think of the sun, sand and sea. Feeling free floating in the ocean and watching the fish swimming amongst the coral. I did not want leave, knowing the decisions I had to make regarding the RCMP and possible lawsuit. As the time return to work approached, anxiety swept over me, and the tightness in my chest returned.

On February 17, 2006, I was at a meeting with Dr. Jupe and the nurse from Health Services Office, a Manitoba Public Insurance Case worker and the RCMP Return to Work Coordinator. At this brief meeting, all eyes were on me. They were all waiting for some indication of thanks from me. I forced myself to remain as expressionless as possible while listening to details of the 'position' in Staffing which was meant to 'accommodate' my medical restrictions. Did they honestly think I would be grateful, after all these years? For me this was too little too late. I looked blankly from person to person as each one was speaking and I showed no emotion. I knew what I had to do. I had to get out of D Division or I would die. I knew I could not handle being there for another day. Dr Jupe commented, "Well, it is important to put things behind us and move forward." I looked at her with angry eyes when I realized that she was hoping I would do what I always did, give in and come back to work. Perhaps she could put this behind her, but I was the one who had been suffering. No, I would not put this behind me, I would move forward out of the clutches of the RCMP. They did not know my thoughts to sue the RCMP in Federal Court and go to the Canadian Human Rights Commission. After this meeting, I had the weekend to think about it. David had come back for a few days from Halifax and although I wanted to be happy, joy seemed an elusive fantasy. I could not find enjoyment in anything. By the time I drove him to the airport on the Sunday, February 19, 2006 I had already made the decision about my next course of action. The stress was affecting not just me, but everyone: all weekend I was cranky towards Nadine and David. I kept thinking of the decisions I needed to make about the RCMP and the possibility of going to the Federal Court in a lawsuit. The pressure was tremendous and only I could ultimately decide what to do; and I had to go back to D Division one more time, on Monday.

On February 20 I went to a new section in Staffing in the hopes I could find a job that would allow me to get to a twenty year pension. The position offered me was that of an assistant to other Staffing Officers doing various patchwork duties. This was an old pattern with the RCMP: I make waves and they offer me crumbs in order to shut me up. I could no longer work for the RCMP as I feared retribution. Any offer from the RCMP at this point was too little too late. I compared my situation to that of a battered wife. One day she just decides 'enough is enough, I am out of here', and leaves. There is no great reason, no specific event, just "had enough." This was my feeling when they offered me the Assistant position.

The recommendations from my therapist were sent to the RCMP Health Services Office but the suggestion for stress leave could only be acted upon when coming from a medical doctor or a person with a Ph.D. I found it unbelievable no one in Dr. Jupe's office would read my reports that clearly indicated 'this woman is on the edge.' I told this news to my therapist who was stunned at the inadequacy of the Health Services Office.

Thankfully, after an appointment with a psychiatrist, as requested by RCMP, Health Services Office had no choice but to keep me on stress/medical leave.

I saw a psychiatrist at the Health Sciences Centre in Winnipeg, Manitoba. I felt that if this physician could not see how close to a breakdown I had come, then there was no hope for me. I told him a brief history of my years of harassment, discrimination, the lengthy grievance, the ultimate failure in the 'accommodation' and the humiliation of my job. I tried not to cry but the tightness in my chest suddenly released and I sobbed, everything pouring out, all the struggles, fears and disappointments. This was a healing opportunity for me. He needed to recognize I required more time to heal before I could make any sound decision regarding my future with the RCMP. I told him, "All I want is the RCMP to leave me alone so that I can think of what I should do, but they won't leave me alone!" I admitted I had thought of suicide and told the truth when he asked, "If you were to do this, how would you do it?" My response was, "My sleeping pills." He asked if I had tried suicide and I said, "No, but what frightens me is I think of it." After our hour appointment he told me the report would be going to Dr. Jupe's office and we would probably not have to meet again. I left the office emotionally drained, worn out with all my inner suffering exposed. I wondered if I was turning into a 'nut bar'. Had I had done my best in explaining what had happened with the RCMP, the harassment and the years of abuse?

His report was sent to the RCMP Health Service Office, and I was called for a meeting to discuss it with Dr. Jupe. She indicated that, according to the psychiatrist, I was unfit for work with the

RCMP at this time and I was on medical leave for two weeks, to be reassessed at that time. This report from the psychiatrist gave my physician the confidence to keep me on stress leave. The phone calls asking for my 'return to the office' stopped. I was glad to be left alone to heal and consider my future, if any, with the RCMP. I felt as though I was hanging on by my fingernails and they wanted me to salute. The only person who knows how much emotional abuse I can take is me. Although people offer advice or solutions, the final decision as to my future was entirely under my control. I will never again work for an organization that does not value its employees. The RCMP officers who were in a position of power had failed to rectify and stop the abuse, harassment and discrimination. It appeared the organization was completely devoid of creative thinking in the 'accommodation' process and grossly neglected the needs of an injured officer. The RCMP will continue to lose members of the Force unless drastic changes in attitude are made. The stress and strain of harassment, discrimination and abuse of power will eventually weaken the organization from within. I hope some day my experiences will help other officers find courage to address these issues and keep their careers. A safe healthy work environment allows employees and employers to listen and learn from each other.

By May I made a trip to D Division to pick up some documents, which I had asked Howard Brandon, Division Representative, to print, regarding RCMP policies. As I drove in to Winnipeg, I noticed my breathing was getting heavy, my palms became sweaty and I felt tightness in my chest. I was having a panic attack. I parked beside D Division and did Lamaze breathing, the long, deep breaths women in labour take to control their pain. It only took a few minutes and it worked. Although I ran up the stairs and went quickly in and out of the building, I considered this an accomplishment. The next time I went to this building was better as I did not have to run, but still had to do the breathing.

As summer approached I took the brave step of having my lawyer refer my case to another lawyer, James Sims, who specialized in Federal lawsuits. James joined the journey with me down the long confusing road to justice. It became his job to forward the two complaints: one to the Canadian Human Rights Commission in Ottawa and the other to a Federal Court lawsuit. I received a letter from Dr. Jupe stating my medical profile changed to a 04, which meant I was unable to work for the RCMP in any capacity and, therefore, the discharge process would begin. Here we go again! By mid-July, I had to go into D Division and be served the Notice of Medical Board, the first part of the Medical Discharge process. This is done when an officer is deemed unfit for duty or has been off work for an extended period of time. Been there done that! This time I had to go into the belly of the beast, D Division, so my new lawyer, James, accompanied me to ensure my legal safety. I appreciated his support.

Those present were my lawyer, Sergeant Glen Ladaut, Corporal Penny Young and myself. After the hour-long meeting, James and I left to discuss the next move. We agreed the RCMP was trying to fire me. I would not let the threat of discharge sway me from my goal. I wanted my Human Rights complaint drafted and sent, and preparation of the documents needed for the Federal lawsuit to begin.

I continued throughout July to prepare my complaint to the Canadian Human Rights and forward the report. I appreciated receiving a call from the office of the Canadian Human Rights asking if I wanted mediation in an effort to resolve the complaint prior to an investigation by the Human Rights Commission. I did, and as I no longer had a job with the RCMP did not trust them. Would you? My lawyer explained this was good: if we were not happy we could end the mediation and an investigation would go forward. Also, filing the Federal lawsuit would not be affected by the outcome of the Human Rights complaint.

My Canadian Human Rights Complaint went to mediation on October 31, 2006. I went into the meeting with my 'stone policeman' face, little expression and no smiling. It was important to take care of my needs in the meeting and any agreement for the future, as the RCMP had certainly failed miserably at taking care of one of their own. No agreement on an amount was reached, and the Federal lawsuit was then prepared and filed early in December 2006. The Canadian Human Rights Commission withdrew my claim pending the resolution of the Federal lawsuit. Perhaps the hope justice would prevail urged me forward despite the fact I could be poor at the end. By early November, I received a call from D Division Health Service office, informing me as per an order from Northwest Region in Regina I was no longer allowed payment for therapy. No surprise the RCMP wanted to cut off any support. Upon my arrival to D division in 1992, I spoke to the RCMP Psychologist who authorized the payments for continued therapy since that date. Despite the policy had specific guidelines, the Psychologist agreed to the importance of being comfortable and feeling safe with a therapist. No matter what happened, I was determined to keep the necessary support systems in place. I had to maintain focus on getting justice and making the RCMP accountable. The final result was not as important as getting to this point in my life. I am thankful I was able to recognize the need to get out of the RCMP while I still had the ability to make clear decisions in recognizing my own frailty, the abuse and discrimination. I was fortunate to get out before arriving at the point where I killed myself, as some officers of the RCMP have done.

December 6, 2006, my Federal lawsuit was filed at the Court of Queen's Bench in Winnipeg Manitoba. The RCMP had thirty days to respond. Let the games begin!

Don't Mess With Me, Man!

IT IS INTERESTING TO NOTE HOW PEOPLE REACT TO the press. in January, 2007 I got a call from my lawyer James, asking if I minded if the Free Press ran my story on the Federal lawsuit. "Go ahead!" I said, "This is great, maybe things will change." The next day it was in the paper and arrangements were made for a follow-up in person interview. I needed to show my lawyer all the documentation for my entire career in order to prepare for the Canadian Human Rights complaint. I brought in my box and two bags of original notes dating back to 1991, from my first detachment in Tisdale, Saskatchewan. James was very impressed with the amount of detail in the documents. He had not realized I was organized in keeping this type of evidence and for that many years and he did not know this was only part of the file. As the Free Press reporter was unable to come to the office in person, due to previous court commitments, the interview was held over the phone. I gave him a brief synopsis of my story and reasons for filing the claim, and had a photo taken. This was a terrifying time for me. I felt watched by the RCMP every moment of every day. My dreams dominated by fears of my home being broken into, of being violated and helpless.

On January 13, 2007 I stared at the picture of me in the Winnipeg Free Press. The accompanying article talked about how I had been a single mother on welfare wishing to provide a better life for my daughter by becoming an officer in the RCMP and how the RCMP had put up so many roadblocks.

The public response was immediate. People began to call my lawyer's office offering support; some were willing to go to court and confirm harassment is happening in the RCMP. On Sunday afternoon I was a guest on the radio talk show, Mike on Crime, on CJOB. I was able to go into more detail on the sexual harassment and discrimination in Tisdale, my injury and lengthy six-year grievance, the abuse and harassment that followed and the failure of the RCMP to 'accommodate'. Although I am a private person, speaking out was empowering. I felt I could do anything. No matter what happened with the lawsuit, my quest for justice was going to succeed. The Canadian public will now know abuse and violation are allowed to continue within the ranks of the RCMP.

After the media attention I needed a break, and felt nervous about leaving my boxes of original documents at my house. For the next week I photocopied every piece of paper I had gathered over the years, a total of thirteen hours of photocopying done over several days. In total, 1875 pages, organized by year and date. When this job was completed, I drove to the lawyer's office with my boxes and gave them to James. My face beamed with a satisfied grin and I said, "If anything happens to me, make sure you kick the RCMP's collective butt with this information." He just laughed. Now I was comfortable in the knowledge a copy of my notes was safe. I did not trust the RCMP. My history with them had made me realize this organization can be dangerous as well as unpredictable.

Eventually the thirty days were up, and the lawyer for the RCMP requested a 'Demand for Particulars', copies of the evidence that supports my allegations in the claim. At home and in the privacy of my bedroom, I opened my boxes of misery, and spread out the coloured file folders spanning my career in the RCMP. I had a sense of sadness seeing all these folders, bulging with papers. If only the RCMP had listened and stopped the abuse years ago. Quietly, I sat down and started looking through the files, preparing dates and times needed for the request for particulars. It took over fifty-six hours to complete this exhausting and time consuming job. Each day I devoted many hours organizing and typing documents to prove the claims of harassment, discrimination and abuse of power. I knew the truth must be told and changes made to the internal structure of the RCMP.

The delays only seemed to add to stress to my life. I was notified March 2007, the RCMP was seeking a Medical Discharge based on physical and 'mental stress.' My lawyer James, sent a letter to the Commanding officer of D Division addressing the mental component and suggesting as there is a Federal Lawsuit in the negotiation stage, this Notice of Discharge will be viewed as continued harassment and abuse of power by the RCMP. The response from D Division was to continue with the Medical Discharge. Here we go again!

My daily life continued to be filled with the 'battle.' Getting the mail every day like everyone else, except for me, there is fear whenever I see a brown envelope or registered letter slip, and my heart tightens. This physiological reaction comes from years of receiving letters from the RCMP which contained bad news for me on my case. Not only have I suffered emotionally but also professionally and financially for past and future revenue of a what should have been 25 to 30 year career, including wages and pension over the approximate length of time I would live. This would have amount to several hundred thousand dollars.

During 2007 the RCMP is preparing the Medical Discharge process against me. The RCMP continued in its failures to take responsibility for the actions of members of their organization. In light of the allegations of corruption at the highest levels in the RCMP, and the Commissioner's integrity questioned by Parliament, how can there be any hope for those seeking help from lower ranks, with less power? When asked to endorse my book, senior officers are reluctant. Their response is usually, "Well, I agree with you but you know how the RCMP works. I still have a family member in the Force." These fears of retribution are legitimate. My journey continues, I am fighting each step of the way in my quest for justice, and I hope others can be encouraged not to give up. Realizing I might be sued for this book has only increased my desire to proceed. If a person has done nothing wrong, then there is nothing for them to fear.

By fall of 2007, the RCMP, facing its own internal challenges with the Commissioner resigning, and the Deputy Commissioner being asked to step down as Human Resource Officer under a cloud of corruption. There are several other lawsuits from officers in the RCMP. A new Commissioner has been appointed, with no police experience. I no longer feel alone and as I watch and wait for a successful conclusion, while the RCMP continues to follow the path of denial on the charges of harassment, discrimination, sexual harassment and abuse of power. Deep in my soul I know whatever happens in the future, taking the risk of speaking out is something I had to do for justice. Was I free? Nope, it would take another three years.

Who Would Have Thought
It Would Have
Turned Out This Way

AS THE MONTHS DRAGGED ON, THE LAWSUIT SEEMED to be on slow and actually stop and I desperately wanted to get on with my life. It was as if the healing was never going to happen. My life was in limbo.

For years restful sleeps were elusive and few, the never ending fatigue of tossing and turning; no sleep and freaky dreams of being chased by unspeakable monsters were none other than the RCMP in disguise. Learning to control my fear of white cars, police cars and brown envelopes was fine when I was awake, but in my dreams, it was a different experience. Old fears surfaced and with the history of the treatment continuing into my present, it became a game of who will blink first. I knew this brain drain had to stop.

It was important to take back my power and look to the future, this I did by writing Women Not Wanted and continuing to take courses towards my Conflict Resolution Degree at the University of Winnipeg.

David thought taking me away from the home front might be a

good stress reliever. Boy, oh, boy I needed to escape to another planet. He booked a quick trip for four days in London, England and three days in Paris, France, 6th to 13th of November. Thank heavens for collected airmiles points. The flight was from Winnipeg to Toronto then to London. We spent three action packed days visiting all the places I had wanted to see again. In Paris, we walked everywhere. Up and down the Champs Elysee. On November 11, 2007, David and I watched the Remembrance Ceremony from the street as newly elected President Sarkozy officiated. There must have been over 2000 Paris police officers and soldiers blocking off the roadway and searching bags. I thought of my job from the 'old days' on highway patrol and the feeling of satisfaction there is in helping people.

People in London and Paris could recognize us as Canadian because we wore bright red cloth poppies with a black centre. After a few days, I spotted other Canadians in the crowds with their bright red poppies. David and I walked to The Louvre, in the rain, in Paris. Yes, it was so romantic. Standing beneath the Eiffel Tower was magical! The pubs are where the locals and the tourists mingle to eat. The menus placed where people can read food choices and prices. I reminded David in Paris there is price for having a drink at the bar, a different price for sitting at a table and a higher price sitting on the patio. Wherever we were, it was enjoyable. As this was winter, it was too cold to be having dinner outside. During our holiday, I had to keep reminding myself this is not a dream! I finally had the honeymoon of a lifetime. Spending time in London and Paris with David was an adventure I had anticipated for years. At the end of the week, I knew the trip was over and it was time to return to reality, the RCMP battle and my book.

Finally, after several weeks, the printers called to say this book was done. I could have one copy, the balance in a few days. I took a copy to show several family members. Within a few days David picked up five boxes and, with the excitement of a five year old, I ripped open the lid, stared at my own eyes looking up from the red book cover and my name in black. At last the voice from inside me was going to be heard. I did not care if I sold one book. I did it! I put my pain into print in spite of the fears of retribution from the RCMP and the useless leaders.

The next day I took a few books to town and gave them away to family and friends. The first visit was to my parents. I glowed with excitement, this book was my experience, growth and a desire to encourage others. Holding onto the past only allows the negativity to fester and destroy the soul. This was the reason for writing the book in the first place, to get the pain on to paper and begin the healing process.

There is no malice intended to anyone, only the facts of my life and career with the RCMP. In fact, this book is a personal reflection of lessons learned: family experiences, personal choices and as a single parenting. I felt there was a need to be accountable and this book is just that. I admitted to having been sexually assaulted; I had relationships with men who were not available; I was going for therapy; and during the struggle with the RCMP, I contemplated suicide. I certainly do not come out looking perfect.

The local book store in Gimli was eager to have copies and have a book launch—I gave them a few copies. On discussing this with James he suggested holding the release of the book as this could affect the settlement negotiation. Feeling a little put off, I agreed waiting until the New Year for the book launch, but no longer. McNally Robinson in Winnipeg was also excited by the concept of the story and the book launch was scheduled for January 28, 2008.

Christmas was coming and I did not want this legal matter ruining another happy and joyous season. To tell the truth, I had to work hard to not allow sadness overwhelm me. David was great in his support and reminded me why I wrote the book -- to find my voice. No, I did not have a perfect past. We all make mistakes in our lives. As parents we may have bad parenting practices but once we learn better skills, our parenting improves.

I sold a few books to friends and sent books to various Members of Parliament in Ottawa in the hope of gaining attention for the next generation of officers. I could not understand the delays by the RCMP lawyer. However, I did understand the client. As time continued to drag, it was costing me money but mostly this chain of doom tied to my ankle was holding me back. I dropped off my book for Roger, James and his assistant. At a meeting with James in December, I met a woman who was an Employment Specialist willing to go to court and testify to the emotional trauma resulting from years of sexual harassment. Her words were moving and I suddenly began to cry, something I had not done in front of James. He was taken by surprise. When I expressed my own surprise, she calmly said "It is hard to heal this wound when people keep picking at it. This would be the lawsuit that won't go away." James gave her copies of the necessary documents to facilitate the report and I gave her the book in order to illustrate my experiences over the years.

James emailed me during the holidays to say the RCMP lawyer wanted a meeting to start negotiations in early January 2008. My concern was the report on the emotional trauma was not completed and I felt it important to have an independent expert witness ready and willing to go to court. Apparently, this report was not required.

Later that week I drove to Winnipeg for a meeting with the Employment Specialist in her office. Her words stunned me, "In all the thirty years I have been doing this, yours is the worst case of harassment I have ever seen. I read your book once to get an idea of what was going on, then read it again and prepared some notes. It made me cry, Sherry, it really did."

It was important to be open and honest about how this battle had affected me, my relationships, my self-esteem, my daily life. It was painful revealing how afraid I was of the answering the phone, getting the mail for fear of a brown RCMP envelope, white cars, police cars and being alone in my own vehicle. During the interview, she was able to better understand my life as a female officer. I was able to explain how the years of stress resulted in three miscarriages, developing Celiac Disease and the strain on the relationships with David and Nadine.

The Book Arrives!
What a Reaction!

AS I LET GO OF THE PAST AND FOCUSED ON MY BRIGHT new future, the dreams did not improve. Even on the holidays under the warmth of the Mexican sun, I wondered if I would ever be happy and free. Something was holding me back and only I was responsible to figure it out.

As January 28, 2008 approached, I was excited about the book. David met me at McNally Robinson in Winnipeg. Some family members and friends were present, having braved one of the coldest nights of the winter. Several classmates from University also attended and showed their appreciation for my effort in identifying workplace violence against women. It was not a concern if or who was watching from the RCMP. I would not be intimidated.

As I was introduced and walked to the podium, I looked at the audience feeling a sense of pride. After the reading, I signed books for those who wanted copies. Several people came up to me at the coffee shop to tell me it was an 'inspiration' and recounted how they would like to change things in their lives. It was truly a surprise at the number of people who knew of or experienced similar harassment and other violence. Some people spoke privately of their own experiences; such as the blue wall of silence within the RCMP, problems of domestic violence by officers, other workplace sexual violence and the silent shame for victims. Basically, each person was pleased the book brought these problems out into the public arena. I could relate to their plight, and hoped for and gave reassuring words to them to not give up. I stressed the importance of self-care and and explained that justice has no time barriers in sexual assault.

This reaction to the McNally Robinson book launch was quite fantastic – much, much better than I could ever have imagined!

The legal battle seemed to drag on forever. I was so sure the release of my book would cause an outrage across Canada but it did not. Although several reporters contacted me for a story, there was some reluctance on their part to go forward. It was not until several months later one reporter actually admitted "if the RCMP can terrorize you, a fellow officer, what will they do to me." His fears were legitimate.

In March 2008, I received a call from the Grievance Section in Regina informing me there were documents which needed to be served on me and could the RCMP come to my home. I did not have to think long for my response, "no." I requested all necessary documents be served on my lawyer, also any correspondence should go to him. He would then contact me. The documents indicated I was to receive official Notice of Medical Discharge as of April 9, 2008. Once again I relied on John French to get some insight for my next move and a few words of encouragement.

Together we met with an officer working at D Division, who gave insight into the RCMP mentality of a select few, "Your book didn't make any difference. Well Sherry, the RCMP wants to destroy you, either force you to commit suicide or ruin you financially."

Reader you can imagine how I felt! The words were like a punch in the stomach, all air seemed sucked out of my chest and a steel like grip around my throat. It was most beneficial such a comment as this was made in the presence of a witness, in front of my friend, a retired RCMP officer.

This statement alarmed me to the core, and I could not shake off the sense of fear and intimidation. What did I do that was so wrong? What have I done that is unforgivable? How can the organization change if they keep bullying the employees? It was essential to start the grievance process for two reasons, one in order to buy some time as the lawsuit was going nowhere in the negotiations, and two, to make the RCMP accountable for their pathetic attempt in the "accommodation" process.

As I sat down with my documents and several boxes of orange file folders, I felt so disheartened at the thought of going through this torment again. It was especially discouraging as the officer in charge of investigating my grievance and the adjudicator were both named in my lawsuit. So much for impartiality as the RCMP investigates its own. In my mind it was hell. I thought, "The same miserable experience day in and day out, is this ever going to really be over?" The only escape from the misery was exercise, which I did regularly. My requests to have a new investigator were ignored by D Division and the Grievance Section in Regina. What else was new?

Working diligently to prepare the necessary documents for another grievance on the Medical Discharge kept me busy. In the morning when I awoke just the thought of opening another orange file, gave me a headache, always aware of time limits and the importance of confirmation for the paper work. At the time I did not realize but slowly I was taking back my freedom and moving on. It was little things, such as not allowing what I felt to be an invasion into my personal space and insisting all correspondence go to the lawyer. I had come to dread turning on the computer. It was a small step to preserve my sanity. It was a bold move, but a necessary one, giving me power which was my voice. Another interesting side note, the realization it is okay to seek help. People want to help.

During this lengthy conflict, I had to battle feelings of being the bad one for standing up for my rights as an RCMP officer. The negotiations seemed to go nowhere, nothing was being presented. From my perspective I felt sorry for the defense lawyer -- it was obvious he had a 'difficult client'. Frustration and disappointment mounted in the months and now years it has taken just to get an official offer! It has been my experience with the RCMP any sign of cooperation is interpreted as a weakness.

By now Reader you may be wondering 'when will this end?' No one can imagine the days and nights consumed with thoughts of the lawsuit and now the impending Medical Discharge. It seemed every night I would wake up at four or five in the morning and my brain was racing, fears of retribution from the RCMP, questions on completing paperwork and my economic future were constantly on my mind. Looking back at this journey and the years of disturbed sleep, it was difficult to get out of bed -- I was so tired. Any struggle has its price and for me it was a heavy cost to my mental and physical wellbeing. It is difficult to explain the physiological reaction constant stress can do to the body. I would encourage others to get professional help when feeling overwhelmed.

Like I said, my salvation was exercise, baking, and sharing coffee with positive friends and family. It was difficult for people to understand what it was like, being under a constant cloud of fear and uncertainty. It did not help the stress when I stepped off a chair in February 2008 and broke my ankle! I had to stay off my feet for a week and I hated it. As David was away with for two weeks, I had to cope with not being able to do anything physical. This did not help in relieving anxiety. However, being desperate for exercise, found a creative solution by propping up my foot, used hand weights and did stomach crunches. It was important to find my voice and sense of being and I did this in many small stages. In retrospect, my participating in the 'Vagina Monologues' as the angry vagina was another step in the process. The Gimli Women's Resource Centre was doing the play as a fundraiser and public awareness of the violence against women.

For me having suffered workplace violence I felt drawn to my part, and with no acting experience, it was a special moment being on stage allowing my rage to come out in a creative yet humourous manner. For years it was like I was in a dark bubble and with my speaking out against harassment, writing the book, doing the Vagina Monologues and planning for a ten mile race, slowly, very slowly I could feel alive again. By trying to reach the goals it was my way of poking holes in that bubble, the small tiny holes where the light of hope was streaming in. Although my ankle put my training behind schedule, I managed to complete the race.

After an official offer finally made in October 2008, it was a matter of many months in getting the details resolved. The importance of accountability weighed heavily on my mind. I remembered the meeting with the RCMP officer and his words of the RCMP wanting to destroy me. Had I done enough? Should I continue to fight for the next three to five years in Federal Court? Financially would I be able to handle the costs involved? Could I mentally and physically cope with the many more years of stress required for Federal Court process? What about my family: husband, daughter and my hopes of ever getting pregnant? Have I let everyone down by not continuing? Am I a failure? All these questions plagued my mind as I wrestled with settling. Part of me was drained, sucked inside out, of any and all energy, thoughts of the threat by the RCMP ever present. Yet, another part wanted to continue all the way regardless of the cost.

I decided to try to attain the twenty-year mark and retire. By letting go of this fight did not mean it was the end. During the months leading up to Christmas, the focus was to help others find their voice to stand up against workplace harassment/bullying, education on respectful workplace and accountability. I realized that by not speaking out made as much sense as ignoring a tumor until it becomes a cancer, all consuming and fatal.

As 2009 approached, I was very much aware of the timeline of my career and the question haunting me. How have I helped the next generation of police officers? Will there be any positive changes for women in the RCMP?

Made it to Twenty Years
and Beyond

IT WAS A DIFFICULT TIME HELPING MY HUSBAND prepare to go overseas for six months. for several weeks he had been traveling from city to city across Canada taking the necessary train- ing, and I felt alone with old fears surfacing. Trying to be supportive and coping with my own worries of his trip, I was told that these are normal feelings for partners of soldiers. Winter finally melted into spring and on April 24, 2009, my twentieth anniversary of becom- ing an RCMP officer came and went with for a sense of vindication but no desire for celebration. My mind was preoccupied with David's departure. After reaching the twenty-year mark, whatever happened with the lawsuit and with that chapter concluded, I was ready for my new life to start. For me it was important to begin this new adventure while David was overseas. I set goals for myself for two reasons, one to keep busy and the other to feel free.

The winter had been long and cold and our drive to the airport was a quiet ride. Both of us needed to focus on our own duties, he had his work and I had the lawsuit to finalize. It is hard to put into words saying goodbye at the airport to a soldier. The love you feel for the person, the hope for a safe journey and speedy return. Of course I cried, knowing he wanted to go so how could I deny him this opportunity. Once I lost sight of David in the airport security screening room, the last few tears rolled down my cheeks. Driving away I waited to hear an airplane roar over head, thinking to myself, "Well, no sense feeling sad, it could be a long three months, time to buy a funny movie." I promptly drove to the nearest shopping mall and bought a movie. Back at the house and in our bedroom, I moved the television stand and DVD player. Every night while David was gone, I put on that funny movie. At first it was to make me laugh, then it became like my goodnight kiss from David because we like to laugh.

Prior to his departure, we had agreed to speak face to face once a week and use the web cameras. From my perspective those conversations were important. I looked forward to Saturday mornings and seeing his face. I would have my morning coffee and he would be getting ready for bed but together we could laugh

On May 19th, 2009, I arrived at my lawyer's office to sign the settlement agreement. Nagging doubts flooded my mind as I read over the details. I signed it knowing this book is my voice and nothing and no one would silence me.

In June the Zumba exercise class wanted to participate in the Relay for Life in Gimli. By joining the exercise class, I found it a pleasant distraction from the stress of the lawsuit and another step in my journey. Not only was I gaining the benefit of exercise but new friendships. The women were energetic and fun to be around. The twenty-four hour relay was physically tiring yet inspiring. I dedicated a candle to David's parents who past-away from cancer when he was young. While at the Relay for Life and standing in the crowds of people watching a Zumba demonstration on the beach, I was approached by a retired RCMP officer. Although I had wanted to avoid any confrontation, I felt whatever he has to say, I can handle it. To my surprise he comments were one of compassion and shock, 'I read your book.' he paused for my reaction and when I simply gave a slight smile, he added 'You had a tough time. I had no idea.' While he spoke, he shook his head in disbelief. Perhaps at that moment, I found another challenge, to begin one of forgiveness and understanding. As summer progressed one more goal was to run the ten-mile road race at the Gimli Icelandic Festival during the August long weekend.

Several weeks later, I received a letter inviting me to participate in the Long Service Medal Ceremony to be presented by newly promoted B. Crusoe. At first I laughed at the irony. I was to be presented with the Long Service Medal by the same man who referred to me as 'Princess of Darkness' and also named in the lawsuit. One has to find the humour.

The three weeks leading up to that day were exciting and terrifying, but as the day approached and with David away overseas, apprehension replaced excitement. On the morning of June 24th 2009, I had hardly slept the night before, all I could think of was, "only four more hours and it will all be over." I was to receive my Long Service medal for 20 years. I had made it. My battle began in 1996 and finally, after all these years, the first milestone of getting a pension, the 20 year mark.

On the way to Lower Fort Gary I stopped to help an elderly man on the highway whose van had a flat tire. He had been on his way to the hospital to visit his wife. After chatting for several minutes, I realized his son and grandson worked in Gimli. For a few moments, it felt like it was the old days back on highway patrol, the good feeling of serving the public. He did not seem to notice I was wearing RCMP breeches, a t-shirt and runners. With the weather being over 28 degrees, the red wool coat would have done me in!

After dropping him off at the car dealership, I arrived at my destination. John and Nadine showed up within a few minutes and the three of us tried to get my belt, boots and spurs fastened correctly. I was aware of the importance for the proper uniform. D Division had sent a follow up email to the invitation indicating any officer

who did not conform to the dress code was not allowed to participate in the parade.

The three of us got on a golf-cart like vehicle and were transport-
ed to the ceremony. I asked where the other officers were getting ready
and shown through an archway along a high brick wall. As soon as
I came around the corner, the majority of the officers turned to look
in my direction. I will never forget the feeling of these stares. In the
eyes of many of the people what I felt was distain. Again, the dreaded
sensation began to build up in my body starting in my hot boots.

Nadine noticed immediately the tension filling the air, the looks
on the faces glaring in our direction. "Mom, what is it with everyone?
Why are they looking so mean? I don't like this at all. This is so scary
Mom, I don't want to be here." I suggested she go wait on the chairs
but her response was quick, "I am not leaving you here alone, no way!"
Deep down I was happy she stayed. I struggled with the belt and after
several minutes an officer, whom I did not know, pointed out the correct placement of the belt. The Sergeant-Major who had the task of in-
suring uniformity, made several comments on my hair and uniform.
'You will not be allowed to go on parade without the proper uniform.
What are you doing with your hair? It can't be down, do not expect to
go on parade looking like that.' He was speaking to me loudly enough
for the thirty or so people to hear.

I sent John back to the car because I had left a clasp in the back
seat. This was the first time I had ever been in the parade uniform with
a 'striped Sam Brown' This is our belt around the waist with a cross
strap over the left shoulder to the right hip and fastened with the clasp
which was currently resting in the back seat of my car. One officer
standing beside me who had also been in Regina in the troop ahead
of me did the kindest thing, - offered to adjust the belt to speed up
the process. Recognizing a co-worker, I said 'hello' and as she walked
by and gave no acknowledgement, felt a sense of sadness. Another
female officer did not even look at me with her response. I had been

their co-worker, friend and fellow officer who was willing to speak up against inequality in the RCMP. Again the disappointing sensation of knowing I had done nothing wrong except demand fairness and a harassment free workplace for all officers. As per usual, the victim is notoriously the troublemaker.

I hated every minute as I waited for John to return, knowing full well the Sergeant Major was looking for anything to stop me from being part of this prestigious occasion. Finally, with less than ten minutes to spare, John arrived. The clasp was fastened and my long blond wavy hair stuffed under the stiff brown Stetson. As John and Nadine left me alone in a crowd of RCMP officers, this was the time of desperation in thinking, "Should I just step out of line and go home?" "Will I faint or get sick in the heat?" "I am too scared to be here?" These questions buzzed around in my brain. As the piper began, we formed a line and marched to the area of the presentation where we were seated in several rows in front of the audience. The recipients went up one by one. For me, the only thing going on in my mind was the counting down, "only thirteen minutes and it is over," only twelve and half minutes and it is all over," kept going through my head until it was my turn to go up and get my medal. Standing in front handing out the medals, a person I quickly recognized, one of the men named in my Canadian Human Rights complaint and Federal Lawsuit. Inside of me was a little voice screaming and yelling in triumph, in praise and pride, "I had made it." After all these years, I got to the 20-year mark on personal strength and perseverance.

Feeling light headed and my eyes brimming with tears, I refused to show any weakness or pain I saluted the man who had referred to me as 'the Princess of Darkness', accepted the medal he placed on my red serge, shook his hand and the other officer standing beside, stepped back, saluted and proceeded back to the row of seats. That feeling of vindication, perhaps even revenge served up cold, realizing this man was forced to acknowledge my service, returned and fortified me. I was never so happy as I was to get the hell away from every one there! I had gone up to a few people to say hello and with the reaction being less than cordial, felt encouraged to leave but even found a bit of satisfaction in that. My Aunt Allie, Wray, John, Nadine and my publicist, Holly, were also present.

It is hard to describe the feeling of accomplishment in standing up in front of the officers knowing some did not want me to participate. It was only later upon David's return on leave in July, while watching the 40th anniversary of man landing on the moon was I able to find the right words. The emotion is best described as the same experience every person who participated in getting man to the moon must have felt on that glorious day in 1969. Pure exhilaration and pride.

On the drive home all I could think of was getting as far away from Lower Fort Gary park as possible. I thought of the old man and his wife and wondered if he got home with his van. I continued with self-reflection on my book and my fight for justice; with questions, am I making any difference for the next generation of RCMP officers? I wasn't sure anymore. Exhaustion took over and once reaching the house, I dragged in my uniform, the box and shoes. Getting out of the hi-boots was a lot harder than getting in! With much pulling and yanking they finally came off. Then I got diarrhea which is a difficult experience and not something one would want while trapped in boots.

At a radio interview to discuss 'Princess of Darkness', I answered the question the best I could, making sure I did not come across as bitter and resentful. I acknowledged the honour of being part of the ceremony with these officers who have strong dedication and are of tremendous value in their service, adding how we are more alike than different, in that we want to maintain healthy and respectful workplaces. I addressed my experience with workplace harassment the importance of encouraging people to speak out, find their voice and the need for accountability in the RCMP. If nothing is learned the behaviour continues. I added how thankful I was for the officers who helped with my uniform, and admitted the 'Princess of Darkness' was not the worst name I had been called.

Nadine said she had "no idea what it was like" for me dealing with workplace harassment until today, catching a glimpse of what I had been experiencing for months and years.

With the twenty-year hurdle over and the mental excitement and fear working up to the ceremony, my body went into relapse mode. I became physically weak with nausea and diarrhea for several days. The fact David had been gone for two months and being alone at night was not an issue, however, old fears resurfaced of retribution from the RCMP's command and control, KGB style of management. It was difficult to listen to the news on the Taser tragedy in British Columbia and shake my head in disappointment at the failure in responsibility. The RCMP continues to be in the headlines with complaints of discrimination, harassment and other unethical managerial decisions.

Several days later news of the settlement being finalized did nothing to ease my mind. Freedom was only a breath away. Again the days wore on and it was important to focus on the positive. Training for the Icelandic 10 mile Road Race in August was an important goal. During the race, I could imagine encouraging words from David, "come on sweetie, push it" It was an exhilarating moment, crossing the finish line over three minutes faster than my best time!

Tears rolled from my eyes and as I through my arms in the air yelled uncontrollably, "I did it, I did it." There was more meaning in those two words than just my best race time. Faces flashed in my mind, David, Nadine their love and pride in my 'never giving up', my cousin and aunt who had lovingly christened me the 'Queen of Light'.

Summer kept me busy with yard work and writing. During the months David was away, I wrote a draft of another book. This one used my imaginative spirit and sense of adventure in creating the characters and plot.

Just a few more days and "I am free" my every morning thought and on August 19 , 2009, a weight lifted from my shoulders. This weight of fear, injustice, inequality and abuse was no longer going to hold me back. I had survived twenty years in this organization in which certain people were less than effective RCMP officers. My goals to attain a pension reached, my voice heard with this book, my freedom to begin a new chapter of life, to encourage others to speak up against workplace abuse and conflict, to find happiness.

I could not personally correct my book back in 2007, the pain was too great. It was like poison from my soul. In releasing the second print I took my power back, editing each and every word, facing each and every ghost. Wow. I decided my work from this day forward, to empower people, especially women. If I have learned one important lesson on my journey it is do not expect anyone to rescue you, the only person who can rescue you from your life, is you.

Anyone can stop the cycle of violence by finding ones voice to create a better life full of success and happiness. This can be achieved both in the workplace and in private life. It is my hope the next generation of RCMP officers have satisfying, healthy and productive careers without violence and abuse from supervisors and the RCMP organization.

Finally, a settlement has been agreed upon and so these events are at last truly behind me. It is only a few days until my husband will arrive home from his overseas tour of duty. As I await his arrival, there is a new sense of purpose, an anticipation of the wonderful adventures still to come. Again, I am thankful. You know the expression the only things in life one really regrets, are the risks not taken and challenges not faced. If nothing changes in your life, will you be happy in six months, five years? Only one person can answer this question. Well reader, what are you waiting for? Find your voice and good luck.

Over the last few years I have had the ability to step outside my personal conflict with the RCMP and question why there so many problems with rank and file and management. I have come to believe the failures of the organization are structural and cultural in nature. It begins at the leadership level when the Assistant Commissioners of each province feel above any accountability accept to the Commissioner himself, no provincial watch-dog or provincial Attorney General to answer to, no union to answer to. The message of being "a law onto one's self" filters down to other senior officers in command. Perhaps it is poor training; frontline officers receive less initial training than almost all big city police forces in this country and are expected to learn on the job or with mentoring, or alternatively the fact that unlike other forces we have no union. This reality is compounded by the RCMP's late arrival in accepting workplace conflict and mediation practices used by other federal government departments. An example of this is my own experience early in my career, what to do if you are bullied by your supervisor and co-workers, what if your supervisor comes to work drunk and wants you to lie to cover his accident, what to do if you are sexually assaulted by a fellow officer in your detachment. In training we were taught not to lie but there was nothing that showed us what to do or to whom to turn for help once these events occurred, and no advice on what to do when one suffers or fears retribution and alienation in a detachment environment.

As of June 18, 2010, the RCMP continues to deal with fall-out issues of public mistrust, misuse of force and failure in accountability. The Thomas Braidwood Inquiry into the tragic death of Mr. Robert Dziekanski identifies systemic problems within the RCMP organization in how it manages its own officers. Other recommendations include creating an independent civilian agency to investigate all police-related deaths and serious injuries within both the RCMP and municipal police offices. In late June 2010, a court ruled the RCMP and federal government were in violation of the Charter of Rights by preventing a union from forming within the RCMP. From my perspective, I view these as positive changes for the organization and for the dedicated officers across the country. There is again optimism for the next generation of RCMP officers.

Glossary

Corporal Wooden	DRILL INSTRUCTOR, REGINA TRAINING ACADEMY
Sergeant Darryl Chilton	SERGEANT IN CHARGE TISDALE DETACHMENT
Corporal Mat	SUPERVISOR
Corporal Sam Jones	SUPERVISOR
Corporal Hank	TISDALE DETACHMENT
Superintendent Kline	OFFICER IN CHARGE SELKIRK SUBDIVISION
Sergeant Laven	SELKIRK RURAL DETACHMENT
Sergeant Dave Edmundson	SUPERVISOR SELKIRK HIGHWAY PATROL
Sergeant Bruce MacKinnon	SELKIRK HIGHWAY PATROL
Corporal Wallen	SELKIRK HIGHWAY PATROL
Dr. Pivot	RCMP HEALTH SERVICE OFFICER D DIVISION
Staff/Sergeant Cullen	SUBDIVISION SELKIRK
Sergeant Moyen	SELKIRK SUBDIVISION
Dr. DeComby	SURGEON
Insp. W. Holland	OFFICER IN CHARGE GIMLI SUBDIVISION
Sergeant Jack Medder	GIMLI DETACHMENT
Inspector N. Neige	(RTD.) INSPECTOR GIMLI
Sergeant Stan Mandrake	DIVISION REPRESENTATIVE D DIVISION
Sergeant Doby	ADMIN/PERSONNEL D DIVISION
Sergeant Kevin Sloan	INTERNAL AFFAIRS D DIVISION
Dr. Tippin	RCMP HEALTH SERVICES OFFICER
Inspector Embrouille	OFFICER IN CHARGE ADMIN. AND PERSONNEL D DIVISION
Inspector Lucy Yorrn	OFFICER IN CHARGE STAFFING AND PERSONNEL D DIVISION

Sergeant Art Raul	DIVISION REPRESENTATIVE D DIVISION
Sergeant Jake Fauxl	GRIEVANCE SECTION D DIVISION
Sergeant Girlie	D DIVISION
Sergeant Sinoffoski	STAFFING AND PERSONNEL D DIVISION
Sergeant Glenna	STAFFING AND PERSONNEL D DIVISION
Stanley Smith	EMPLOYEE ASSISTANCE DEPARTMENT D DIVISION
Assistant Commissioner	COMMANDING OFFICER OF D DIVISION T. SMITH
Assistant Commissioner	COMMANDING OFFICER OF D DIVISION FEATHERSTONE
Inspector Victor Belling	OFFICER IN CHARGE COMMERCIAL CRIME D DIVISION
Staff/Sergeant Allan MacDougal	COMMERCIAL CRIME SECTION D DIVISION
Staff/ Sergeant Adam Storm	SUPERVISOR COMMERCIAL CRIME, D DIVISION
Corporal Joy	COMMERCIAL CRIME OFFICER D DIVISION
Staff/Sergeant Wray Bradford	COMMERCIAL CRIME SECTION D DIVISION
Harold Front	STAFFING AND PERSONNEL D DIVISION
Tim Skavinski	PROFESSIONAL STANDARDS & EXTERNAL REVIEW OTTAWA DIRECTORATE
Commissioner Mark Jones	COMMISSIONER OF RCMP OTTAWA
Sergeant Craig Noman	DIVISION REPRESENTATIVE D DIVISION
Sergeant Lucas	TRAINING BRANCH D DIVISION

Superintendent Jerry Kayen	OFFICER IN CHARGE HUMAN RESOURCES NORTHWEST REGION REGINA
Inspector Ezra Adder	OFFICER IN CHARGE STAFFING AND PERSONNEL D DIVISION
Chief Superintendent B. Crusoe	D DIVISION
Doctor Jupe	RCMP HEALTH SERVICE OFFICE D DIVISION
Sergeant Wilma Reading	RETURN TO WORK COORDINATOR D DIVISION
Inspector Devon Simpler	OFFICER IN CHARGE ECONOMIC CRIME SECTION D DIVISION
Sergeant Howard Brandon	DIVISION REPRESENTATIVE D DIVISION
Sergeant Glen Laudet	MEDICAL DISCHARGE PROCESS D DIVISION
Corporal Penny Young	MEDICAL DISCHARGE PROCESS D DIVISION
Doctor Fixet	RCMP PSYCHOLOGIST D DIVISION
Doctor Reader	RCMP PSYCHOLOGIST F DIVISION
Roger Bond	LAWYER 1994 TO 2005 WINNIPEG
James Sims	LAWYER 2005 TO PRESENT WINNIPEG